WHAT
DO WE KNOW
ABOUT
HISTORY?

WHAT
DO WE KNOW
ABOUT HISTORY?

Philip Steele

Author Philip Steele
Consultant Peter Chrisp
Illustrator Dan Crisp

DK LONDON
Project editors Kat Teece, Manisha Majithia
Senior art editor Ann Cannings
Managing editor Jonathan Melmoth
Managing art editor Diane Peyton Jones
Production editor Dragana Puvacic
Production controller Magdalena Bojko
Jacket designer Ann Cannings
Jacket and Sales Material Coordinator Magda Pszuk
Deputy art director Mabel Chan
Publishing director Sarah Larter

DK DELHI
Editor Niharika Prabhakar
Project editor Radhika Haswani
Designers Nehal Verma, Rushil Pradhan
Senior art editor Nidhi Mehra
Managing editor Monica Saigal
Managing art editor Romi Chakraborty
Jacket designer Rashika Kachroo
DTP designers Sachin Gupta, Jagtar Singh
CTS manager Balwant Singh
Production manager Pankaj Sharma
Project picture researcher Rituraj Singh
Senior picture researcher Sakshi Saluja
Creative head Malavika Talukder

First published in Great Britain in 2023
by Dorling Kindersley Limited
DK, One Embassy Gardens, 8 Viaduct Gardens,
London, SW11 7BW

The authorised representative in the EEA is
Dorling Kindersley Verlag GmbH. Arnulfstr. 124,
80636 Munich, Germany

Copyright © 2023 Dorling Kindersley Limited
A Penguin Random House Company
10 9 8 7 6 5 4 3 2 1
001–333901–Aug/2023

All rights reserved.
No part of this publication may be reproduced, stored in or introduced into a retrieval system, or transmitted, in any form, or by any means (electronic, mechanical, photocopying, recording, or otherwise), without the prior written permission of the copyright owner.

A CIP catalogue record for this book
is available from the British Library.
ISBN: 978-0-2415-9956-3

Printed and bound in UAE

For the curious
www.dk.com

Contents

| 6–7 | How do we find out about the past? |

Ancient world

10–11	Where did early humans live?
12–13	What did Stone Age people do all day?
14–15	Who built the first cities?
16–17	Why did the Egyptians make mummies?
18–19	Where was the kingdom of Kush?
20–21	How did metal change life?
22–23	Who was the first Chinese emperor?
24–25	Why were Phoenician ships so good?
26–27	How was ancient Greece ruled?
28–29	How did the Persian Empire rise and fall?
30–31	What happened in the Colosseum?
32–33	Who led the first Indian Empire?
34–35	Were there pyramids in the Americas?
36–37	How was the Pacific first explored?

The Middle Ages

40–41	When did religions start?
42–43	Which city was once called New Rome?
44–45	What was the Silk Road?
46–47	Who were the barbarians?
48–49	Were all Vikings raiders?
50–51	Why did Slavs build sunken homes?
52–53	Could anyone become a knight?
54–55	How quickly did Islam grow?
56–57	Who were the best horse riders in history?
58–59	What is a Chinese dynasty?
60–61	Who were the samurai?
62–63	Which Korean dynasty lasted 505 years?

64–65	Who built temples in Southeast Asia?
66–67	How rich was Mansa Musa?
68–69	How did Zimbabwe get its name?
70–71	Who are the Indigenous Peoples of North America?
72–73	Which Aztec city was in the middle of a lake?
74–75	Who built Machu Picchu?

The exploration age

78–79	Was there anything Da Vinci couldn't do?
80–81	When was Europe's age of exploration?
82–83	When did Europeans arrive in North America?
84–85	Which sultan became The Magnificent?
86–87	Who built the Taj Mahal?
88–89	How did the First Australians live off the land?

Empires and revolutions

92–93	How was the USA created?
94–95	Why did French people rise up in 1789?
96–97	What was the Underground Railroad?
98–99	What work did children once do?
100–101	How much of the world did Europe colonize?
102–103	Can a country go to war with itself?
104–105	When were trains invented?

The modern world

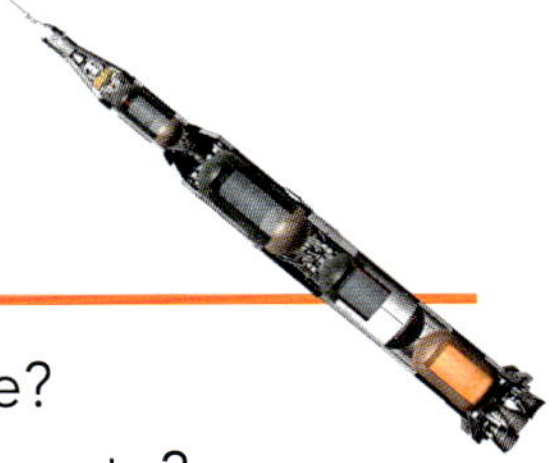

108–109	What was trench warfare?
110–111	How did women get the vote?
112–113	Why did Russians revolt in 1917?
114–115	Can money be worth nothing?
116–117	Who were the dictators of 20th-century Europe?
118–119	How was World War Two fought?
120–121	How did India get rid of British rule?
122–123	Can sitting down change the world?
124–125	What was the Cold War?
126–127	What was the Space Race?
128–129	What is a pandemic?
130–131	How can we make history?

132–133	Answers
134–137	Quiz your friends!
138–139	Glossary
140–143	Index
144	Credits and acknowledgements

Find out who I am on page 78.

? Quick quiz

Test your knowledge! Look out for the "Quick quiz" boxes throughout this book to see how much you've learned. You'll find some of the answers on the pages, but you may have to look up or give your best guess for the others. Turn to pages 132–133 for the answers.

WHAT IS HISTORY?

How do we find out about the past?

Throughout history, people have left things behind that can tell us about their lives – shoes, toys, weapons, and more. Some people made art that we can study. Others wrote things down in languages that were lost, and are now waiting to be deciphered.

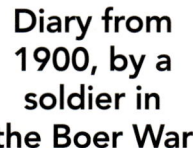

Diary from 1900, by a soldier in the Boer War

The Earth is about 4.5 billion years old. Humans have only been around for about 315,000 years.

Word of mouth
We can learn about people who didn't use writing, or whose writing has been lost, by hearing stories they passed on. You can learn about your own family's past, too, by asking older relatives.

Archaeology
The study of things from the past is called archaeology. Gold jewellery or iron swords are exciting to look at, but old bones or even rubbish heaps hold clues about history, too.

Ancient treasures
An artefact is an object made by humans. Many artefacts are lost over time – wood can rot away, and metals are melted down for reuse. But some remain. Soil can build up over them, until they are dug up.

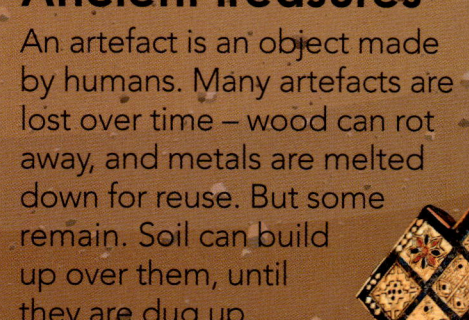

Royal game from Ur

Books

Writing
From shopping lists to books, many people leave behind writing. We can use different pieces of writing to build a picture of the past.

Digital media
You can find all sorts of history facts online. But not everything online is true, so it's helpful to use sites that are trustworthy, such as museum websites.

Where can I go to learn all about history?

The different historical sources on these pages can often be found under one roof, at a museum. Activities at museums might include dressing up or making models.

Mughal painting

Medieval Norwegian tapestry

Art
Paintings, tapestries, and photos can show clothing, food, or daily activities. Buildings are another type of art left over from the past.

? Quick quiz

1. What does an archaeologist do?
2. What is an artefact?
3. Is all information found online true?

See pages 132–133 for the answers

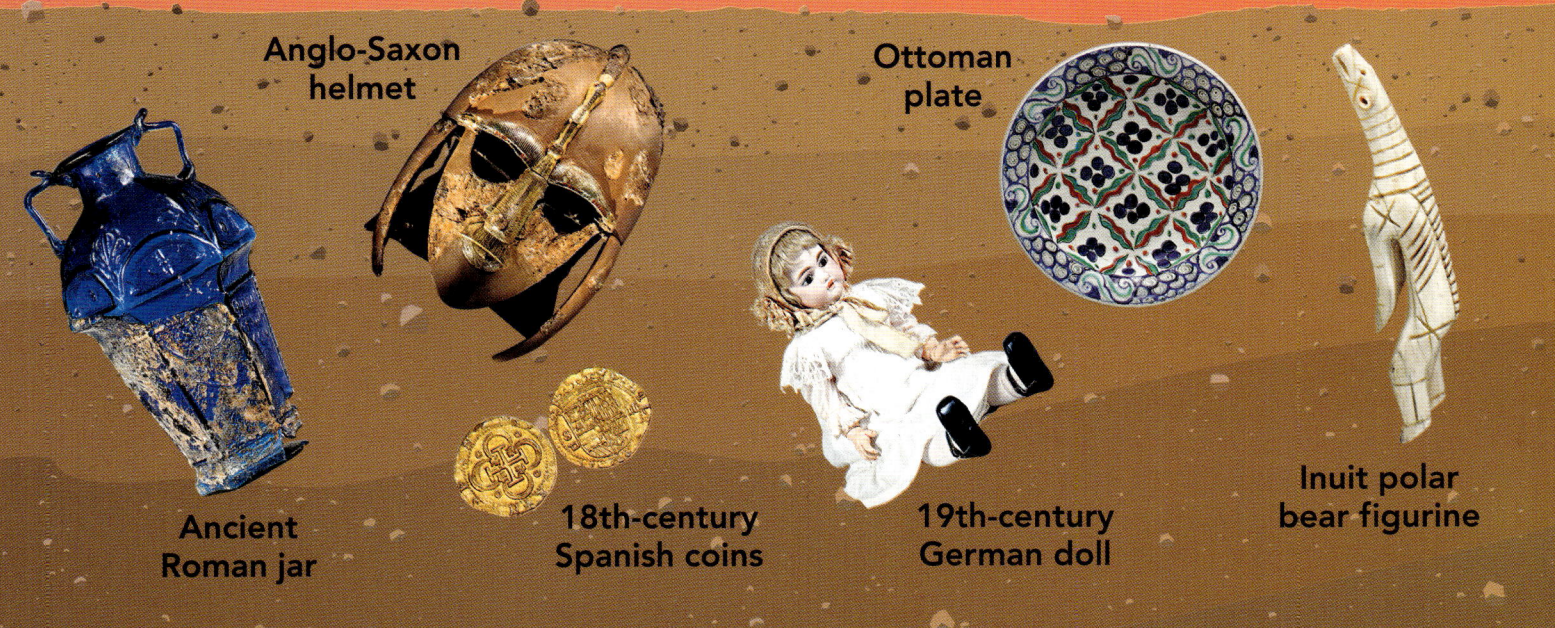

Anglo-Saxon helmet

Ottoman plate

Ancient Roman jar

18th-century Spanish coins

19th-century German doll

Inuit polar bear figurine

Ancient world

Early humans were often on the move, as they followed wild animals to hunt. Learning to farm meant that they could settle in one place. Villages grew into towns, towns into cities, and cities into nations and empires.

ANCIENT WORLD

Where did early humans live?

The first humans lived in Africa about 315,000 years ago. Over time, groups of them began to leave the continent by foot, reaching Asia and beyond. The things they left behind give us clues about where they settled.

Europe
European cave paintings date back to more than 30,000 years ago, and often show animals. But humans were in Europe long before this. A 54,000-year-old human tooth was found in France.

Cave painting of lions, Chauvet Cave, France

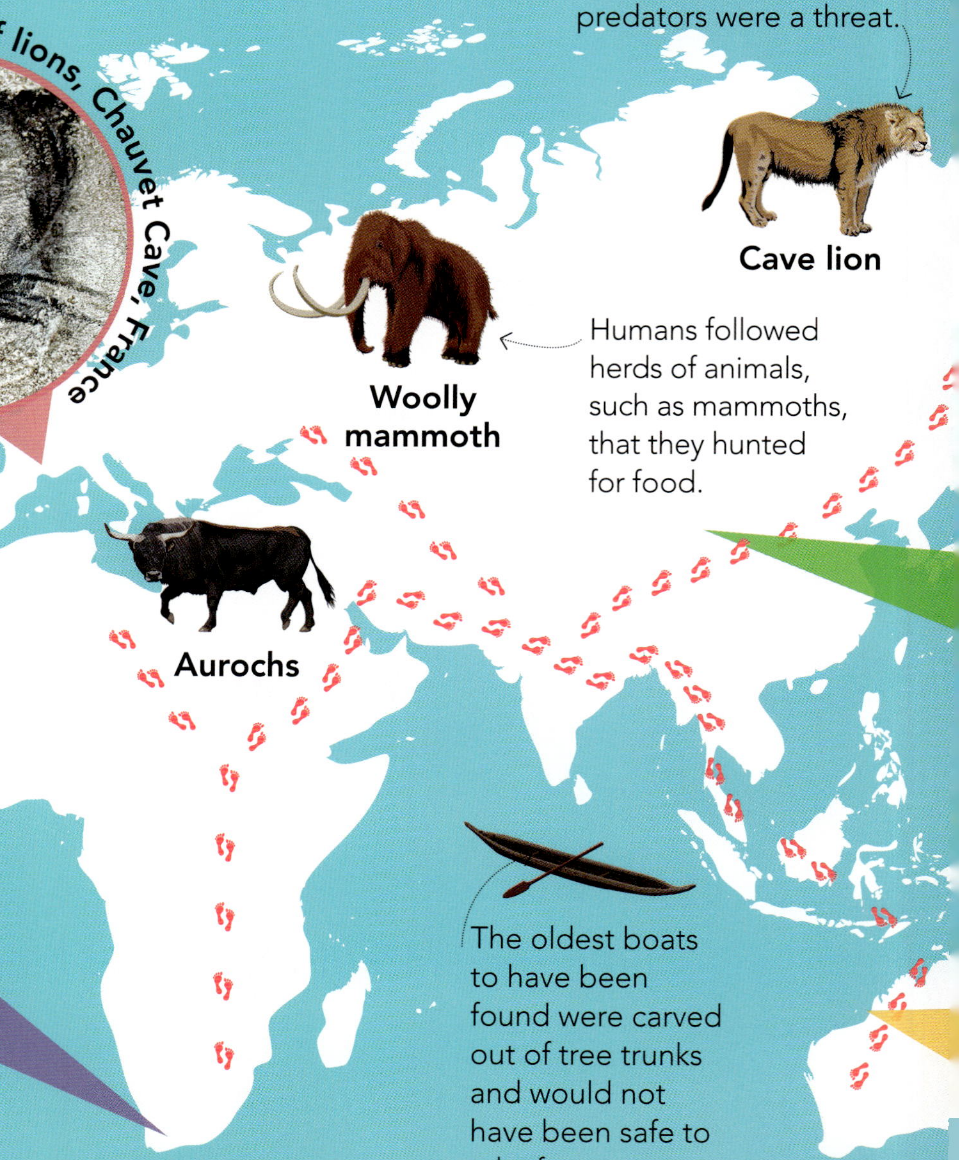

Woolly mammoth

Humans followed herds of animals, such as mammoths, that they hunted for food.

Cave lion

Cave lions and other predators were a threat.

Aurochs

The oldest boats to have been found were carved out of tree trunks and would not have been safe to take far out to sea.

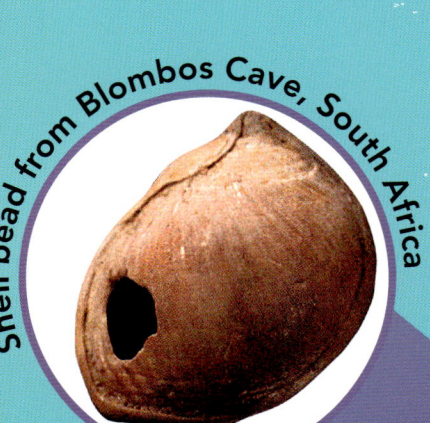
Shell bead from Blombos Cave, South Africa

Africa
Human bones have been discovered in Africa that are more than 300,000 years old. Art and artefacts found there include beads from about 75,000 years ago.

Who came before humans?

Long before humans left Africa, other close relatives had also migrated, or moved away. Two of these species, the Neanderthals and the Denisovans, lived at the same time as early humans, and some had children with them.

? *True or false?*

1. Early humans fought the dinosaurs.

2. The first humans lived in Asia.

3. Many humans today are related to Neanderthals and Denisovans.

See pages 132–133 for the answers

Land bridge

Humans probably crossed into the Americas when falling sea levels left dry land between Siberia and Alaska, 26,000 to 19,000 years ago.

Smilodon

Ochre pigment from Xiamabei, China

Asia

Finds in Asia include paint from about 40,000 years ago, in the form of ochre pigment. This mixture of clay and other minerals comes in red, yellow, or brown, and was probably used for art.

The Americas

Footprints of adults and children in White Sands National Park, USA, date back to more than 20,000 years ago. But some archaeologists think that humans arrived in the Americas much earlier.

Australia

Carpenters Gap rock shelter was used by humans from as long as 51,000 years ago. Finds there include bits of the world's oldest-known stone axe with a handle, from 44,000 to 49,000 years ago.

What did Stone Age people do all day?

The Stone Age was the long period before metal was used. People made things from stone, bone, or wood. Until farming began, food had to be found in other ways. And people still found time to make art.

Crafting tools
People made axes, knives, and wood or animal-hide (skin) scrapers. Hard stones, such as flints, were flaked and chipped into shape using other rocks.

Moving megaliths
European Stone Age people used huge stones called megaliths to build stone circles, burial chambers, and more. The structures were made between 6000 and 1200 BCE.

Painting caves
Some cave paintings may have been part of rituals that people thought would help them in some way, such as during a hunt. Paint was made with ochre, soot, or chalk.

The stone circle of Stonehenge, UK, was put up between c.3100 and c.1930 BCE.

Finding food

People had expert knowledge of where to find food in the wild, such as roots and berries. Sharp weapons were used for hunting, and farming began in around 12,000 BCE.

Where did Stone Age people live?

Shelters were made from local materials, such as wood, stones, mud, or mammoth tusks. Movable tents could be crafted from animal skins, which were useful when people needed to follow wild herds for hunting.

Making clothes

The hide and fur of a hunted animal were used to make cloaks or tunics. Other parts of the animal could be used, too – bones were made into needles, and guts into thread, for sewing the clothes.

Using fire

Fire was needed for warmth, light, cooking, and burning away trees to clear land on which to live. A fire could be started with sparks from a flint and dry sticks.

? *True or false?*

1. A megalith is a large stone.

2. Stonehenge was built in 4000 BCE.

3. Farming was invented during the Stone Age.

See pages 132–133 for the answers

14 ANCIENT WORLD

Who built the first cities?

A few settlements grew into the first cities from around 3500 BCE. As well as streets and homes they had palaces and temples. Some cities began ruling nearby people, becoming larger states and even empires.

Mesopotamia
This land, between the Tigris and Euphrates rivers, in what is now Iraq, was home to various cities. The Babylonian civilization grew here, from the city of Babylon.

Mesopotamian people worshipped their gods in stepped temples, called ziggurats.

Babylon

This text describes a great wall being built around Babylon. It is written in one of the earliest-known writing systems, cuneiform, which is from Mesopotamia.

How did farming help cities grow?

As farmers, people no longer needed to follow wild herds of animals for food. So, they began to settle. In lands where crops grew well, such as those around large rivers, enough grain could be grown to feed lots of people, and cities began to develop.

Indus Valley

Cities such as Harappa and Mohenjo-Daro grew up around the River Indus, in what is now Pakistan. They thrived from 2600–1900 BCE, and traded (swapped) goods with other lands.

Mohenjo-Daro

Houses had flat roofs, bathrooms, sewers, and drains.

❓ Quick quiz

1. What was a ziggurat?
2. Which writing system's name means "wedge-shaped"?
3. Which two rivers did Mesopotamia lie between?

See pages 132–133 for the answers

The cities of the Indus Valley had their own system of writing – but we still haven't managed to translate it!

Indus-Valley children played games with dice and marbles. They also had wheeled toys to push along the ground, like this wheeled pottery model of a bird with a ram's head.

16 THE ANCIENT WORLD

Why did the Egyptians make mummies?

A wrapped-up mummy

The ancient Egyptians believed that when someone died, they would have a new life in the world of the dead, called the afterlife. The body of the person needed to be preserved in a life-like form and prepared for the journey. This process was called mummification.

Removing the organs
The body was carefully washed. The internal organs were cut out to stop the body from decaying too quickly. The brain was hooked out through the nose. Only the heart was left in the body, as it was thought to be the centre of intelligence.

Drying out
The body was then placed in a mixture of salts called natron for 40 days to remove all the moisture.

Giving it shape
Now, the empty body was filled out with cloth, or stuffed with sawdust or sand.

Wrapping in linen
The skin was rubbed with scented oils and coated with resin, a sticky substance from trees. The body was then wrapped in linen bandages. Protective charms were attached to the strips of cloth.

Mummy case of Lady Takhenmes, made in about 747–656 BCE

In total, the process of mummification took 70 days.

Coffin cases were made from layers of papyrus or linen, covered in plaster.

Placing in a case

The mummy was placed inside a human-shaped coffin case. Some of these were beautifully painted, with life-like faces, pictures of gods and goddesses, and magic spells. The coffin cases were placed for protection inside a stone box called a sarcophagus.

What happened to the organs?

Some of the organs were stored in special containers, called canopic jars. The lid of each jar was shaped like the head of the god that protected the organ. The brain was thrown away as the Egyptians did not think it was important!

Intestines
Qebehsenuef, a falcon, held the intestines.

Lungs
Hapi, a baboon, kept an eye on the lungs.

Stomach
Duamutef, a jackal, guarded the stomach.

Liver
Imsety, with a person's head, guarded the liver.

? *True or false?*

1. The ancient Egyptians also made mummies of animals such as cats, crocodiles, snakes, and baboons.

2. The Egyptian god of mummification was called Osiris.

See pages 132–133 for the answers

Where was the kingdom of Kush?

Egypt was not the only state of ancient Africa. Kush, Punt, and Axum lay to the south of Egypt, while the Nok civilization grew up in what is now Nigeria. The people from these lands left behind artefacts including sculptures and monuments.

Nok
People who lived around Nok from about 1500 BCE were farmers. They smelted iron from about 100 BCE, and made terracotta heads that may have shown their gods or ancestors.

Terracotta head from Nok

Figure of a Kushite pharaoh of Egypt

Kush
This state was on the Nile, in Sudan – with a capital city at Meroë. Kushites traded with the Egyptians, who ruled Kush from 1550–1070 BCE. Kushites later ruled Egypt, from 747–656 BCE.

? Quick quiz

1. Which great river ran through Kush and Egypt?
2. What is terracotta?
3. Where was the Nok region?

See pages 132–133 for the answers

Egyptian art showing a queen of Punt

Punt
From c. 2500 BCE, Egyptian ships sailed down the Red Sea to trade with this kingdom, which may have been in what is now Sudan. The people there lived in reed huts built on stilts. They sold gold, incense, ivory, and animals.

Axum
This monument from Axum, in Ethiopia, honours the Axum King Ezana, who became a Christian and conquered Kush. Axum also came to rule parts of Sudan and Yemen. From c.100–940 CE the kingdom traded far and wide.

What goods did Axum trade?

Plenty of gold could be found in the rocks of Axum, and this was mined and turned into coins. Foreigners came to buy goods including salt, ivory, and gems, such as emeralds (pictured).

Kings and queens of Kush were buried in the Pyramids of Meroë, in modern-day Sudan.

20 ANCIENT WORLD

How did metal change life?

One of the biggest steps forward for humans was the discovery that heating an ore (a rock containing metal) melted the metal inside. Metals could then be used to make strong farming tools, weapons, and more.

Bronze in Europe
From about 2150 BCE, bronze axes were being used in Western Europe to cut down trees to clear farmland. Bronze is a mixture of copper and tin.

Metal through time
Metals were first used in different parts of the world at different times. These dates show when historians think they were first used in the world.

5500–4000 BCE
Copper
Copper began to be used for items including axe heads (pictured) at the end of the Stone Age.

c.4500 BCE
Bronze
Mesopotamians used bronze c.2,000 years before Western Europe. This mirror is from ancient Egypt.

2000 BCE
Iron
Iron was first taken from ores at around this time in Asia, for items such as sickles (pictured).

Round shield
Pendant
Sword
Axe head
Bracelet

Roundhouse
Many Bronze and Iron Age Europeans lived in roundhouses. These might have been built out of stone, wood, and packed earth, and had a straw roof and central fire pit.

Iron Age Celts

From around 1100–100 BCE, ironworking peoples known as Celts lived in Europe. They made beautiful, patterned bronze, iron, and gold metalwork.

True or false?

1. The first iron that people used came from space.
2. Bronze is a mixture of iron and tin.

See pages 132–133 for the answers

Detailed hilt

Bronze helmet
This Celtic headgear is thought to have been thrown into a river as an offering to a god.

Sword

Armlet

Bracelet

Ironworkers
Iron is stronger than bronze, and it cannot easily be melted to pour into moulds. In an Iron-Age smithy, it was heated to make it softer, then hammered into shape.

22 ANCIENT WORLD

China united
Chinese civilization grew up around the Yellow River from about 3000 BCE. China had many different states and rulers in its early years, but Qin Shi Huang was the first to unite it.

The Great Wall
Northern China was already protected from the attacks of neighbouring lands by sections of wall and earthworks, or long mounds of soil. The new emperor joined them together into one, strong wall.

One currency
Qin Shi Huang replaced China's different currencies, or types of coins, with one currency. One of these coins had a hole in the middle so it could be stored or counted on a rod or string.

Who was the first Chinese emperor?

By 220 BCE China was split into seven states that fought for control over each other. In 221 BCE, one of the states, Qin, finally conquered the other six. The leader of this new empire was Qin Shi Huang.

An empire is a large group of lands brought under the rule of one person or government.

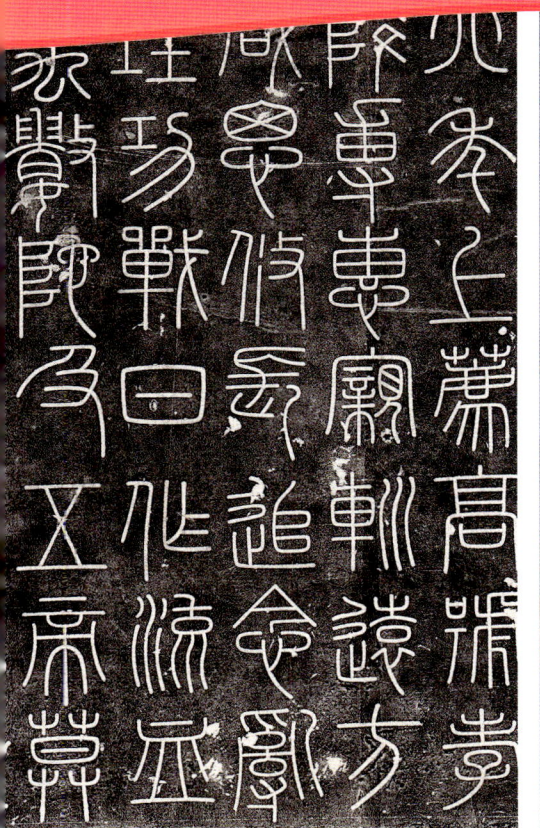

Chinese writing
Writing had been used in China since before 1200 BCE, but the characters were often different across the states. Under Qin Shi Huang, 3,000 characters were chosen to be used throughout China.

Roadworks
A network of roads was built across the land by Qin Shi Huang. It was now easier to send messages and transport goods, such as food – and to move troops if the empire needed defending.

Tomb army
Qin Shi Huang died in 210 BCE. He was buried with a guard of 8,000 life-sized pottery soldiers. Many historians think the statues were made to defend him in the afterlife.

What were some important inventions in ancient China?

Many clever inventions originated in ancient China. These include silk-making, porcelain (fine china), and cast iron. Paper, like the sort we use today, was first made from hemp or rags in China in about 105 CE, or even earlier.

Making paper

? Picture quiz

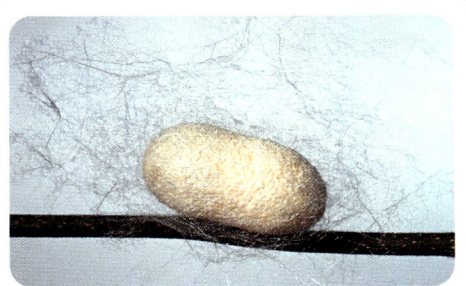

Which creature does silk come from?

See pages 132–133 for the answers

Why were Phoenician ships so good?

By around 1250 BCE, a civilization had grown up on a narrow strip of the eastern Mediterranean coast. This was Phoenicia, and its people made money from the sea – by building ships to take goods across the ocean to trade with other lands.

Trading voyages
The Phoenicians sailed all around the Mediterranean Sea. They founded ports on the coast, where they could trade goods. Cádiz, in Spain, was a Phoenician port.

Ivory
Ivory, or elephant tusk, was used in many places to carve ornaments, such as figures. Phoenician merchants traded both tusks and carved ivory.

Locator

EUROPE
ITALY
Cagliari (Caralis)
Palermo (Panormus)
SPAIN
Cádiz
Tunis (Carthage)
AFRICA

Which was the most powerful Phoenician city?

The Phoenician city of Carthage came to control most of Spain and the North African coast. In 246 BCE war broke out between Carthage and its main rival, the growing republic of Rome. The Carthaginians fought Rome at sea and in Italy itself, but in 146 BCE Rome finally won, and Carthage was destroyed.

? Quick quiz

1. Which modern Spanish city was a Phoenician port?
2. What was the dye called Tyrian purple made from?
3. Which modern country has a cedar tree on its flag?

See pages 132–133 for the answers

Purple dye
Roman emperors sought out purple-dyed Phoenician cloth for their royal clothes. The dye was collected from sea-snail slime in the Phoenician city of Tyre.

GREECE

Sail power
Merchant ships had a single, square sail. If there was no wind to blow the ship along, oars could be used.

Cedarwood
Cedar trees grew on the mountain slopes of the Phoenician homeland. Their wood was strong and made sturdy boats.

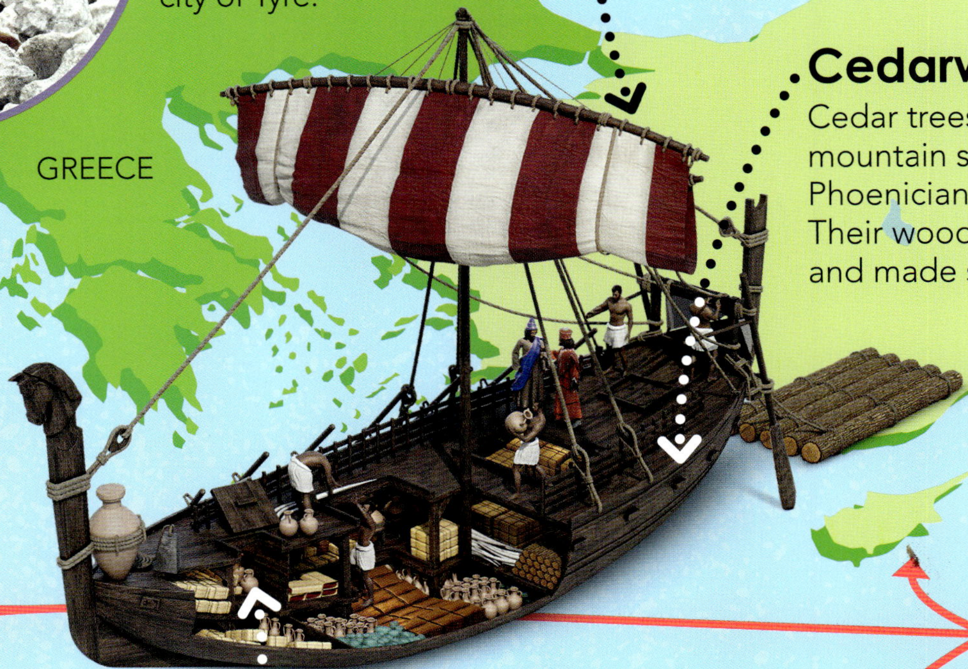

Tyre
ASIA

Cargoes
Ships were built to carry bulky cargoes, or loads. Goods ranged from fish to cloth and perfume. Timber could be towed behind.

26 ANCIENT WORLD

How was ancient Greece ruled?

The ancient Greeks lived in many small states, often ruled by a single leader or small group. But from about 500 BCE some states, such as Athens, began to be ruled differently – by an assembly of the people. This type of rule was called democracy.

Men who refused to attend the Athens Assembly were marked with red paint and fined.

Modern democracy
The word "democracy" means "rule of the people". In today's democracies, people vote for local or national leaders or parties to represent them in government, and to vote on important decisions.

Ballot (vote) box

The Pnyx
From 507 BCE, 40 times a year, the Athenian Assembly met on this hill. Speakers stood at the top, where they could easily be seen.

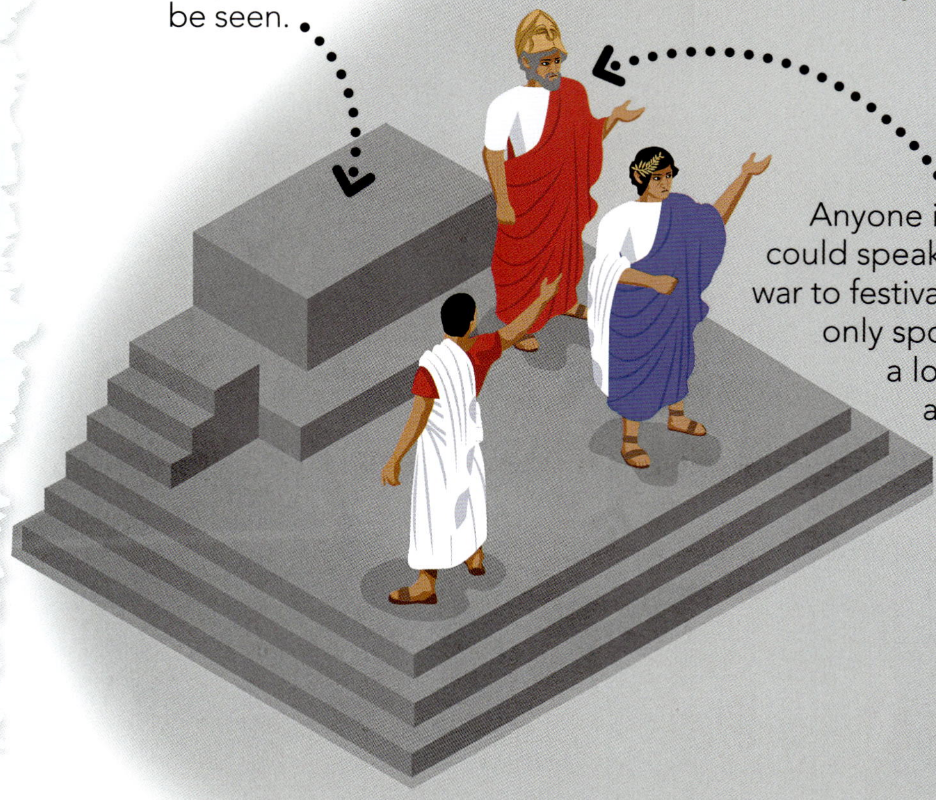

Speakers
Anyone in the Assembly could speak on topics from war to festivals. Most people only spoke if they knew a lot about a topic, as they could be shouted down otherwise.

Voters

About 40,000 men could attend the assembly, but most meetings numbered about 5,000. They voted for actions by raising their hands.

How did they vote people out?

The Assembly could vote to banish people from Athens for 10 years. They did this by writing down the person's name on an old shard of pottery. The shards were collected and counted.

Great thinkers

A philosopher is someone who thinks about big questions, such as how to treat people fairly. Many famous philosophers came from ancient Greece.

Quick quiz

1. Who could be part of the Athens Assembly?

2. Was Greece a single country?

3. What does "democracy" mean?

See pages 132–133 for the answers

ANCIENT WORLD

Tributes to the King of Kings
Every corner of the Persian Empire sent wealth to the ruler – the king of kings. This wealth was used to enlarge the empire, for example, by paying soldiers to invade new lands.

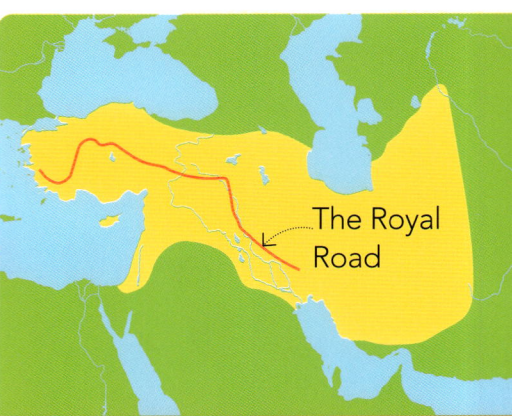

The Royal Road

Clever governing
Governors looked after each part of the empire. They sent long-distance messages via horse riders along a network of roads. King Darius I (c. 550–486 BCE) rebuilt the 2,500-km-long, ancient Royal Road.

How did the Persian Empire rise and fall?

The Persian Empire began in 550 BCE. Centred in modern-day Iran, it grew to stretch all the way from Egypt to South Asia. This vast empire tried to conquer Greece – which led to its downfall.

Struggles with Greece
Darius I (below) tried and failed to conquer the neighbouring civilization of Greece. His son, Xerxes I (518–465 BCE), took up the same cause, but his armies were pushed back, too.

Who is Ahura Mazda?

The Persian kings, and many other Persians, worshipped one god – called Ahura Mazda. They believed that he battled forces of evil in the world. This religion is called Zoroastrianism, and it is still followed today.

Quick quiz

1. Which great empire was ruled by the king of kings?

2. Who was the first Persian King to invade Greece?

3. What was the name of Alexander's new city in Egypt?

See pages 132–133 for the answers

The Hellenistic world
Alexander continued to grow the Macedonian Empire. He built new cities such as Alexandria (above), in Egypt, and spread a Hellenistic, or Greek, way of life. He was remembered as Alexander the Great.

Philip II of Macedonia

Alexander the Great

A new enemy
Philip II of the Greek state of Macedonia (382–336 BCE) conquered much of Greece. When he died, he left his son, Alexander (356–323 BCE), in charge.

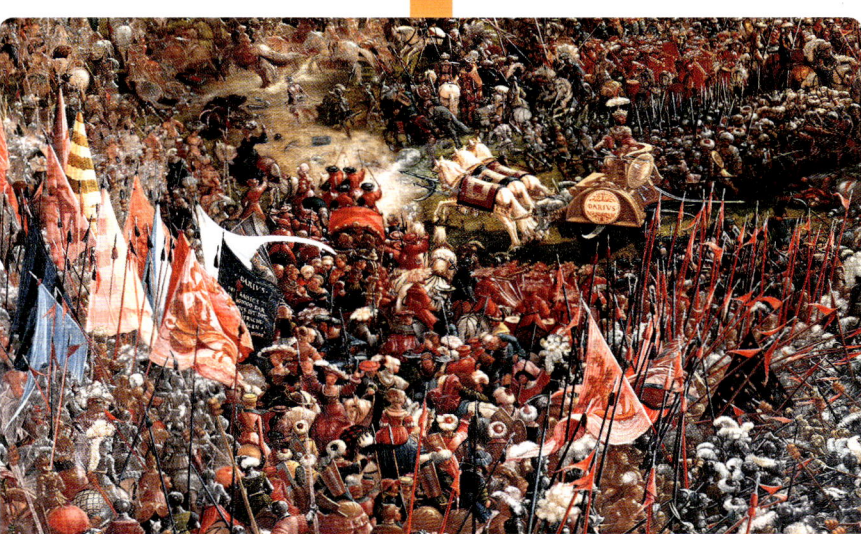

Battle of Issus
In 334 BCE Alexander led his army into Asia, where he met the Persian king, Darius III (c. 380–330 BCE), in battle at Issus. Alexander won this battle and more, eventually absorbing the First Persian Empire into his empire.

ANCIENT WORLD

What happened in the Colosseum?

By 80 CE Rome was at the centre of a huge empire, and home to a million people. A huge new amphitheatre (a round stadium) had just opened – the Colosseum. Crowds of people flocked to watch what went on inside.

Gladiators
Well-trained fighters, called gladiators, fought each other, or wild animals, with deadly weapons. They were often slaves or criminals, who could become famous by winning.

Spectators
The Colosseum could hold a crowd of 50,000. They roared and cheered as they watched gladiator fights – and ate snacks, such as salted peas.

Structure
There were four tiers of spectator seating. Beneath the arena were passages, rooms for gladiators, and cages for the wild animals.

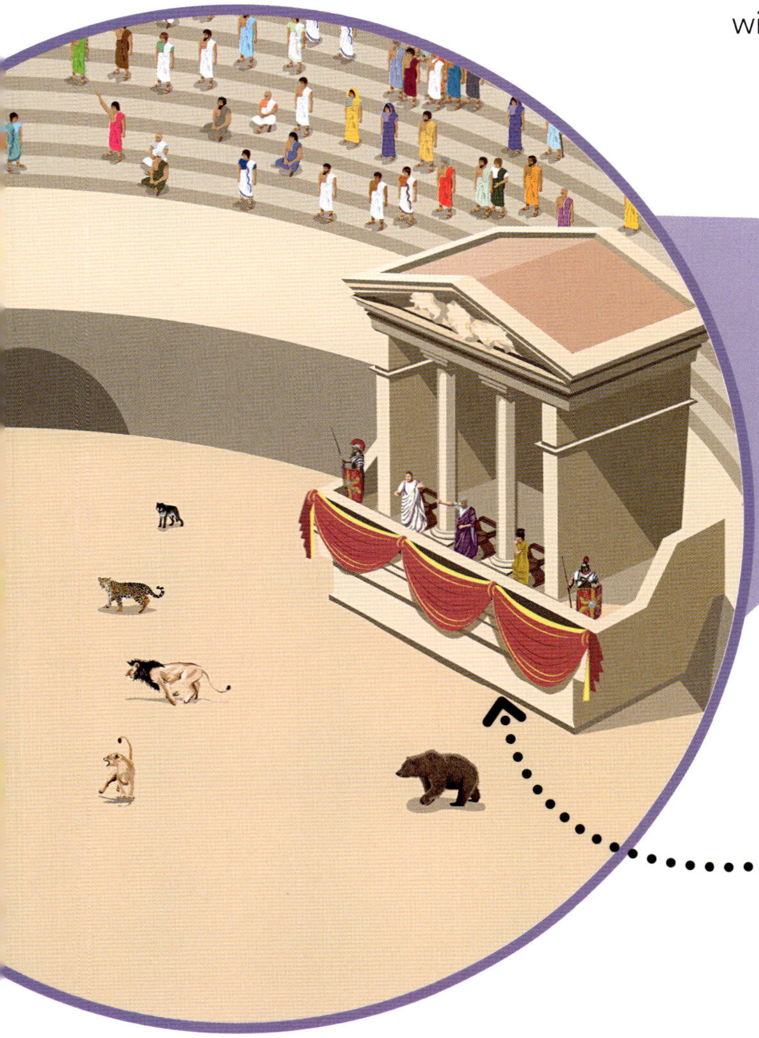

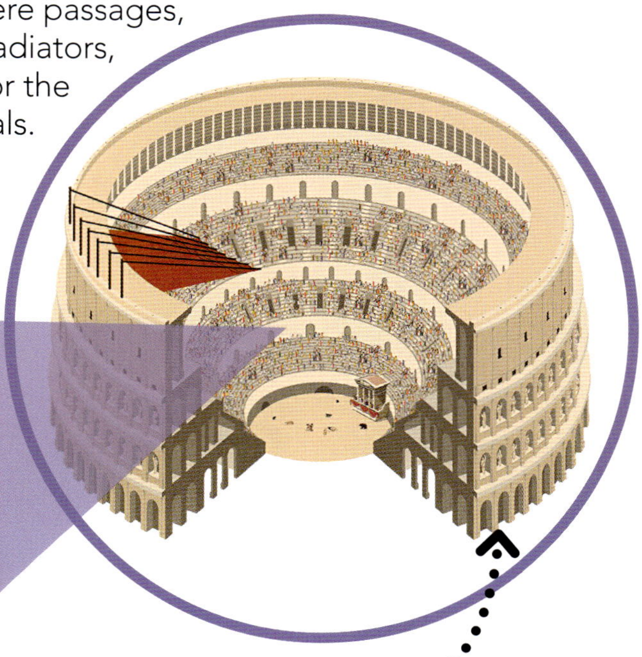

Outer wall
The outer wall was 48 m (158 ft) high, with 80 entrances at street level. Its arches were probably decorated with statues.

Emperor's box
The person paying for the games, called the sponsor, was often the emperor himself. He decided if a gladiator should be killed at the end of a fight.

What was Rome's oldest stadium?

The Circus Maximus was Rome's oldest stadium, and could hold 250,000 spectators. It was famous for its games, festivals, long-distance foot races, mock battles, and exciting horse and chariot races.

? Quick quiz

1. Where were the lions and tigers kept?

2. What were people trained to fight in the arena called?

3. How many spectators could fit in the Colosseum?

See pages 132–133 for the answers

32 ANCIENT WORLD

Who led the first Indian empire?

The Indian subcontinent was home to many different kingdoms when Chandragupta Maurya set out to conquer an empire. In 322 BCE he succeeded, becoming the first person to join large parts of India into one empire.

The Mauryan Empire c. 270 BCE

Chandragupta Maurya
Under Chandragupta (322–297 BCE), the Mauryan Empire grew to cover northern India. New roads were built, which made it easier to trade goods. This helped make the empire wealthy.

? Quick quiz

1. What is a stupa?
2. What is the state emblem of modern India?
3. Which religion has the most followers in India today?

See pages 132–133 for the answers

Ashoka's lion capital, or column's head, from Sarnath is the state emblem of India.

What was the Sanchi Stupa?

A stupa is a dome-like, Buddhist monument. The Great Stupa at Sanchi, in India, was originally built by Ashoka. People believe it contains some of the ashes of Buddha.

Ashoka

Chandragupta's grandson, Ashoka (c. 304–232 BCE), is said to have turned to Buddhism because he wanted there to be no wars. Under his rule, the religion spread far and wide.

Buddhism

This religion is based on the teachings of a man who became known as the Buddha, who wanted to end human suffering. Buddhists try to help end suffering, too.

Pillars of Ashoka

Ashoka had pillars of stone put up in many parts of his empire. They were carved with Buddhist rules for everyone to read and follow.

34 ANCIENT WORLD

Were there pyramids in the Americas?

Across the Atlantic from the pyramids of Egypt, huge, stepped pyramids were built in North, Central, and South America. They were built by different civilizations, and were often used for religious ceremonies.

Chichen Itza
Home to a number of pyramids, this city was built by the Maya people in Yucatán, Mexico. It was a living city from about 600–1200 CE.

Wriggling snake
Twice a year, at the start of spring and autumn, a trick of the light brings this stone to life. The setting sun creates shadows, which make it look as though Kukulcán the Feathered Serpent is creeping down the steps.

Where did the Maya live?
The Maya civilization grew up across Central America. It included what is today Guatemala, Belize, parts of Honduras and El Salvador, and a large area of Mexico.

Temple of Kukulcán
This nine-layered pyramid, known as El Castillo, is topped by the temple of the plumed serpent god, Kukulcán. It was built over earlier pyramids.

? Quick quiz

1. Do descendants of the Maya still live today?

2. Which pyramids were older, Egyptian or Maya?

3. What lies underneath El Castillo?

See pages 132–133 for the answers

Clever maths
There are 91 steps on four sides and one platform at the top. Together, these add up to 365 – which is the number of days in a solar year.

Hidden secrets
El Castillo is built over a hidden cenote – a water-filled cavern. The Maya believed that cenotes were entrances to the Underworld, known as Xibalba.

Who were the Olmecs?
The Olmec civilization was the first that we know of to spring up in Mexico. The Olmecs may have been the first in the Americas to use writing, in c. 900 BCE. They left behind giant, carved stone heads, which may show their rulers.

How was the Pacific first explored?

The Pacific is the world's biggest ocean. From about 1500 BCE, the part of it now known as Polynesia began to be settled by seafarers from East Asia. They travelled in simple canoes at first, but over time they built better boats for longer voyages.

Where did the Polynesians sail to?

The Polynesians made longer voyages than anyone had before. They settled on Pacific islands from the west, such as Tonga, to the east, such as Easter Island (above).

Well-built boats

The first Polynesian boats were canoes carved out from tree trunks, with wooden bars, called outriggers, either side for balance. Later came double canoes, like this one.

Moving around

Double canoes could reach 20–30 m (65–98 ft) long. They could carry 100 people, plus plenty of useful settler items, such as fruit plants and pigs.

Sails
Pandanus leaves or coconut palms were woven into sails. Boats could cover 150–250 km (93–155 miles) in one day.

The Māori of New Zealand are descended from Polynesians who reached the country in c.1250.

? Quick quiz

1. Which is the Earth's biggest ocean?

2. Where are the Polynesian people thought to have first come from?

3. Today, Hawaii is a part of which country?

See pages 132–133 for the answers

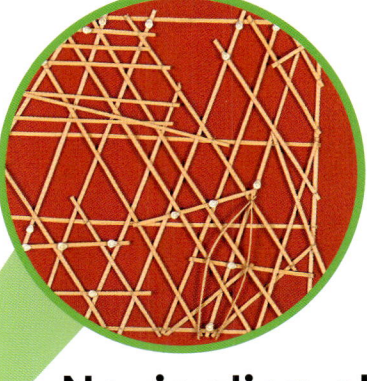

Navigation chart
Criss-crossed stick charts like this could show the location of winds or ocean currents. Shells marked where islands were.

Double hull
Lashing together two hulls made the boats stronger and more stable in the open ocean.

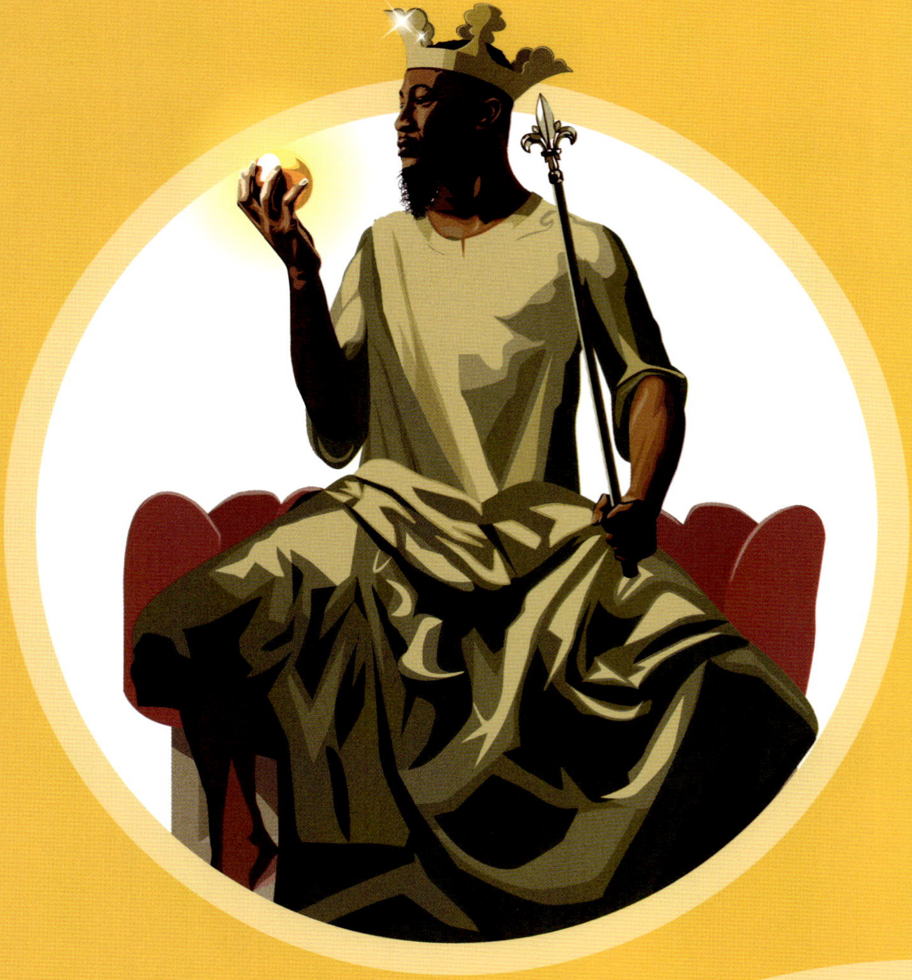
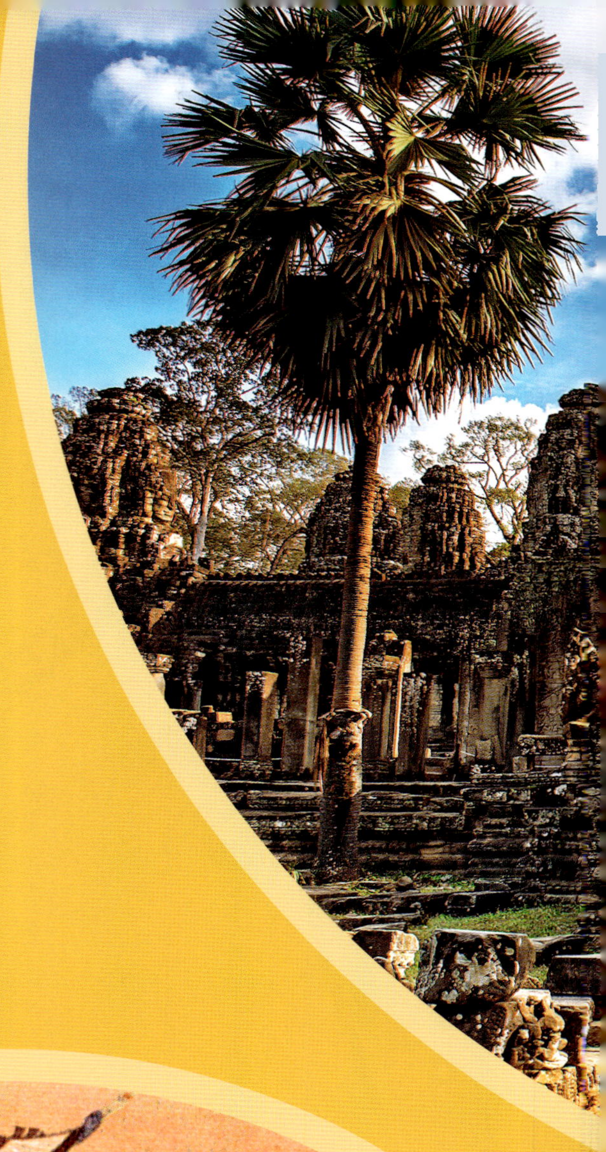
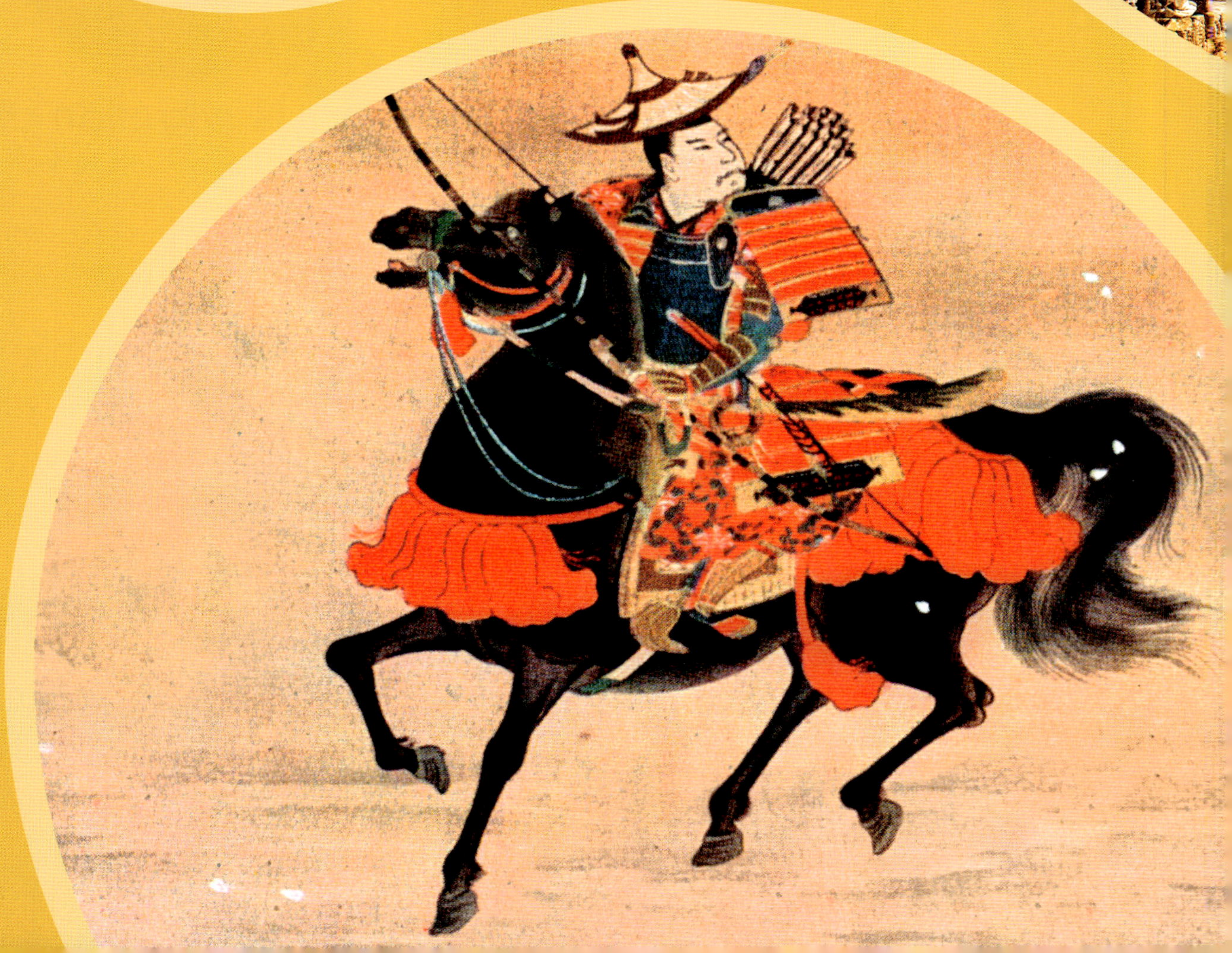

The Middle Ages

The period of history extending from about 500 to 1400–1500 CE is traditionally known as the Middle Ages. During this time, luxury goods were traded along the Eurasian Silk Road, and civilizations arose in Central and South America.

When did religions start?

Throughout time, humans have been faced with many puzzles. Why is there a Sun? What happens when we die? People began to believe that spirits or gods were behind it all. Some sets of beliefs became religions, such as these.

Judaism
Judaism is the ancient religion of the Jewish people, said to be about 4,000 years old. Its prophet Moses was believed to have been given 10 commandments by God.

Sikhism
Sikhism began in India with the teachings of Guru Nanak (1469–1539). Nine other gurus came after him. Sikhs believe in one God, and in a life of virtue (goodness).

Buddhism
The Buddha is believed to have been born in Nepal in about 564 or 480 BCE. Buddhists follow his teachings.

Christians, Jews, and Muslims believe in one God, and respect the prophets Abraham and Moses.

Hinduism
Hindu beliefs grew up in India about 4,000 years ago. Hindus believe in rebirth, and that life is sacred. Many worship one god (Brahman), but in different god and goddess forms.

How many gods can a religion have?

One god
Many religions worship a single God, who is sometimes believed to be the creator of the universe and all living things. This type of religion is called monotheism.

The Christian God is on the left in this painting.

Many gods
The worship of more than one god is called polytheism. More than 2,000 gods and goddesses were worshipped in ancient Egypt.

The Egyptian gods (left to right) Seth, Sekhmet, Osiris, and Isis

Christianity
Jesus (c. 4 BCE–30 CE) was a Jewish religious teacher. Christians believe that he was the son of a single God, sent to live as a man, and that he died on a cross but came back to life.

Islam
Muslims believe that Muhammad (born c. 570–632 CE) was the messenger of a single God. Muslims must pray, fast (not eat for a period), give to charity, and go on a pilgrimage.

? Quick quiz

1. What is polytheism?
2. How old is Judaism?
3. Which religion has the most followers in the world?

See pages 132–133 for the answers

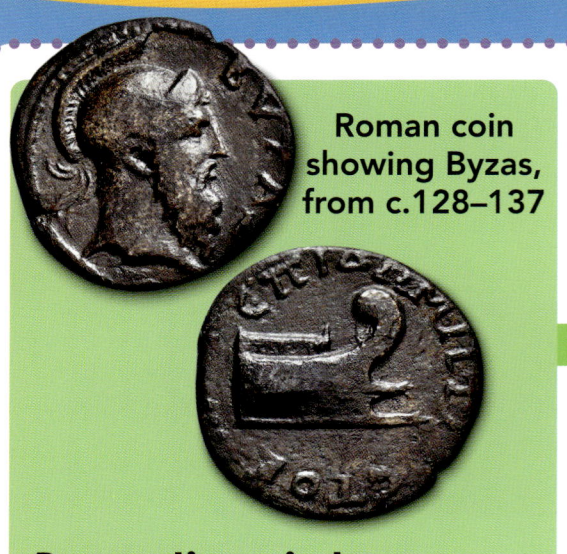

THE MIDDLE AGES

Roman coin showing Byzas, from c.128–137

Byzantium is born
This city on the eastern edge of Europe was founded in about 667 BCE by the ancient Greeks. Myths told that Byzas, the son of a Greek king, led them there. Rome captured the city in 73 CE.

New Rome
In 324 the Roman Emperor Constantine renamed Byzantium "New Rome" – though people began to call it Constantinople, after him. From 330, he made it the capital of the Eastern Roman Empire.

Emperor Constantine

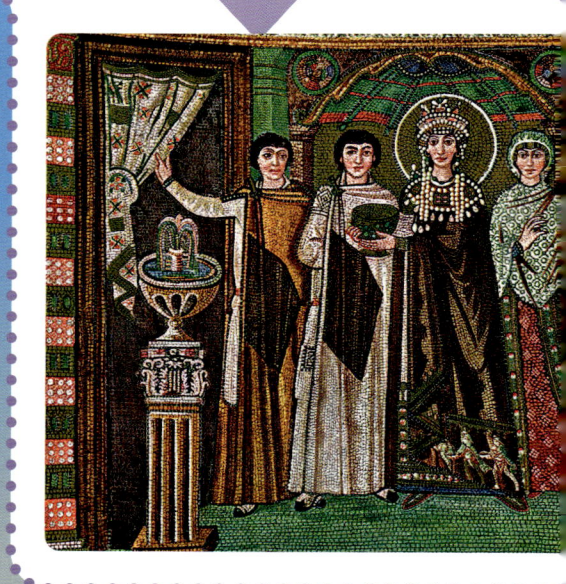

Which city was once called New Rome?

Istanbul has had many names, and has been part of more than one empire. After being taken over by the ancient Romans it was renamed New Rome. It later became the capital of their eastern lands, the Byzantine Empire – which outlasted the western part of the Roman Empire by 1,000 years.

? Quick quiz

1. Who founded Byzantium?
2. Which Roman emperor was Constantinople named after?
3. In which modern country is Istanbul?

See pages 132–133 for the answers

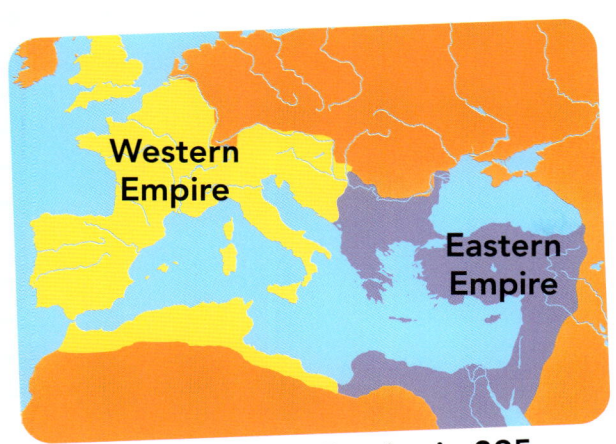

The Roman Empire in 395

West and East Rome
The Western Roman Empire fell apart in the 400s, after being attacked by enemy peoples. The East tried but failed to reclaim the lost lands.

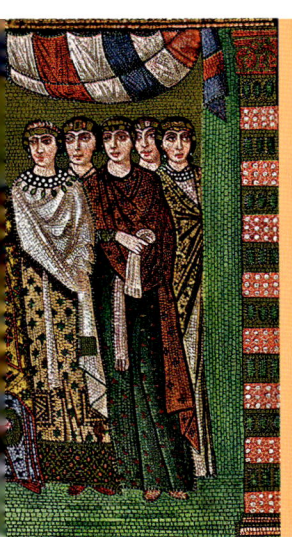

The last Roman capital
In the 500s, Emperor Justinian I and Empress Theodora ruled over a splendid city with new laws. There was the great cathedral of Hagia Sophia, towering city walls, chariot racing, and aqueducts.

The fall of Constantinople
The Byzantines lost lands to Arab and Turkish invaders. In 1204 Christian Crusader knights sacked Constantinople. In 1453 the city fell to the Ottoman Turks.

Istanbul
Under the rule of the Ottoman Turks, Constantinople became a Muslim city, known as Istanbul. The Hagia Sophia cathedral became a mosque.

Hagia Sophia

MEDIEVAL WORLD

Marco Polo
One of the most famous travellers along the Silk Road was a Venetian merchant called Marco Polo, who wrote about his travels in the 13th century.

Trading centres
Towns along the routes grew into large, bustling centres of trade. These cities, such as Samarkand, in modern-day Uzbekistan, became some of the richest and most powerful in the world.

Venice

Rome

Constantinople

Samarkand

Baghdad

Western goods
Goods travelling eastwards included glassware, gold and silver, domesticated animals, and animal furs and skins for making clothing and leather.

East meets West
Constantinople (now Istanbul in Turkey) was the capital of the Byzantine Empire, and was seen as the meeting point between Europe and Asia. It was one of the largest trading centres along the Silk Road.

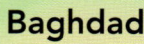

Guest houses
Travellers could break their journey at guest houses, or inns, called *caravanserai*. There were stables for their animals and secure warehouses for their goods.

Around 750 to 850, ships sailed from Arabia and Persia to China and the islands of Southeast Asia.

● Trading centres

What was the Silk Road?

The Silk Road was a network of trading routes connecting Europe to China from around 130 BCE to 1453 CE. European countries were eager to buy luxury goods from Asia, which was the richest part of the world for thousands of years.

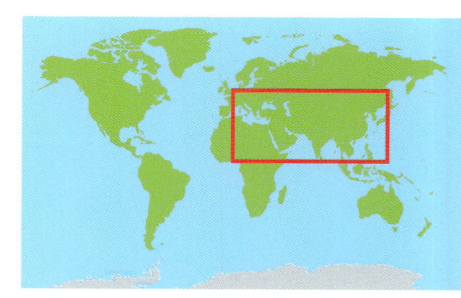

The Silk Road routes covered a distance of about 6,500 km (4,000 miles).

Caravans

Merchants travelled together in groups, called caravans, to stay safe from robbers. Camels were used to carry goods, as they could easily cross the challenging terrain, which included deserts, grasslands, and mountainous areas.

Kashgar

Chang'an

The capital of ancient China, Chang'an (now Xi'an) was considered the starting point of the Silk Road. During the Tang period (618–907), Chang'an was one of the largest cities in the world.

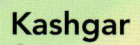

Chang'an

Silk weaving was a Chinese invention.

Chinese goods

Although silk was the most valuable item, China also exported tea, ivory, jade, and porcelain. Spices from India and southeast Asia were brought to China along southern sea routes.

South Asian exports included scented sandalwood, and spices such as cinnamon and nutmeg.

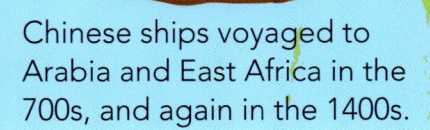

Chinese ships voyaged to Arabia and East Africa in the 700s, and again in the 1400s.

How did ideas spread along the Silk Road?

Ideas and information spread along the Silk Road as much as goods. Travellers relayed news, told stories, and played music. Pilgrims and monks spread religious faiths, such as Buddhism, and towns grew into multicultural cities. Dangerous diseases, such as plague, were also passed along these routes.

? Quick quiz

1. How long was the Silk Road?

2. How many years did it take Marco Polo to get to China from Venice, Italy?

3. Where did the Silk Road begin?

See pages 132–133 for the answers

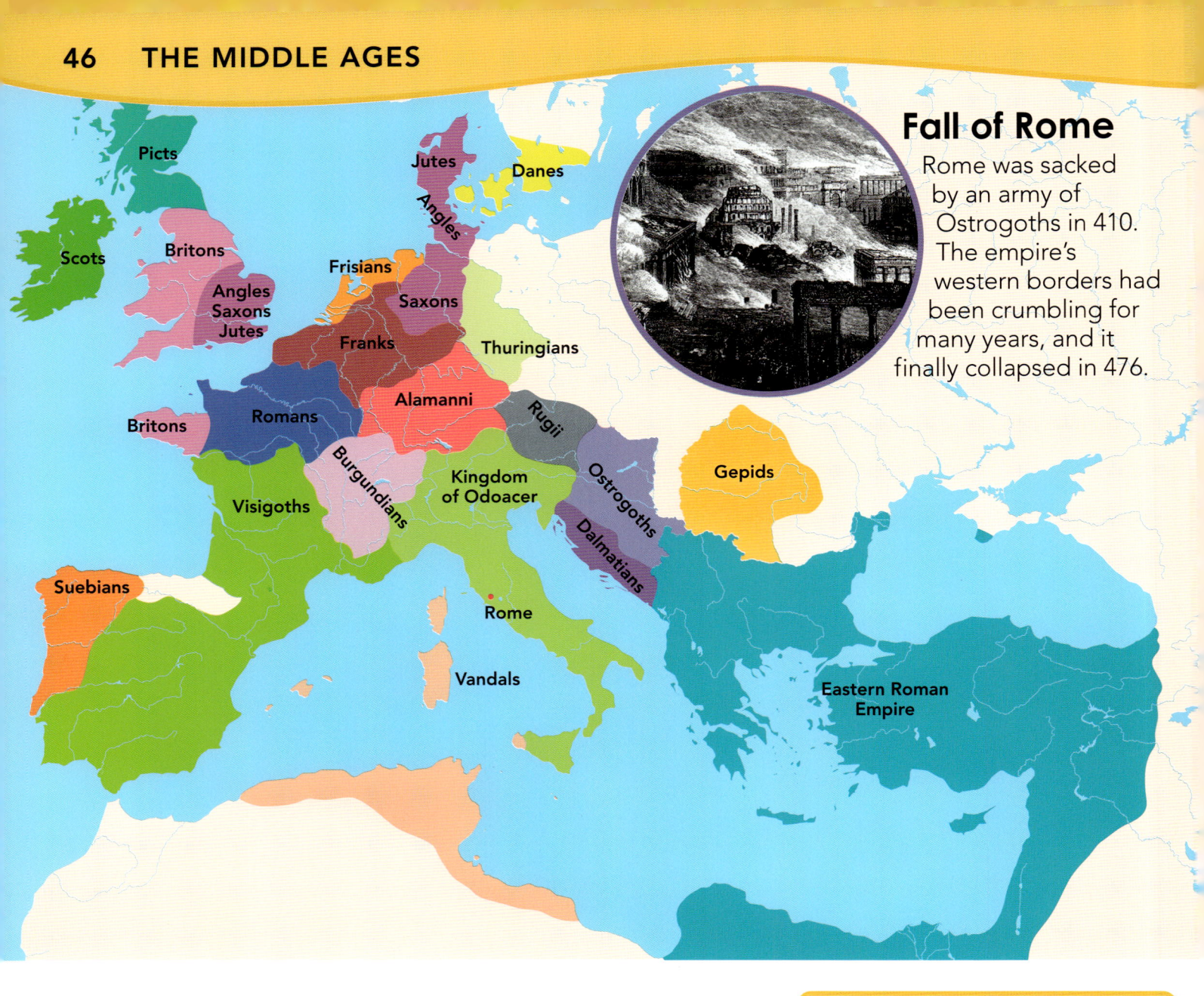

THE MIDDLE AGES

Fall of Rome
Rome was sacked by an army of Ostrogoths in 410. The empire's western borders had been crumbling for many years, and it finally collapsed in 476.

Who were the barbarians?

The Romans called the people in neighbouring lands "barbarians". They spoke similar languages, which later became English, Dutch, and German. After Rome fell, the barbarians took over the lands it had ruled in Western Europe.

Who were the Franks?

The Franks were a people whose kings ruled France and Germany. Charlemagne (747–814, above) founded an empire that took in much of Western Europe.

Mainland Europe
The Ostrogoths, Visigoths, Vandals, Lombards, and Burgundians began ruling areas of Italy, France, and Spain after Rome fell. This crown was made by the Visigoths in Spain.

Britain
In Britain, Roman rule ended in 410. Angles, Saxons, Jutes, and Frisians founded small kingdoms. Celtic Britons held out against the invaders in mountainous Wales.

Ireland
The Irish began settling in western Scotland. They brought their Gaelic language to parts of Scotland, along with their artistic skills – which can be seen in the picture above, from a Bible.

What is a runic alphabet?
Runes are stick-like symbols, used as letters by some European peoples from c.150 CE. Different groups of people used different sets of runes. They were mostly replaced by Roman letters as Christianity spread.

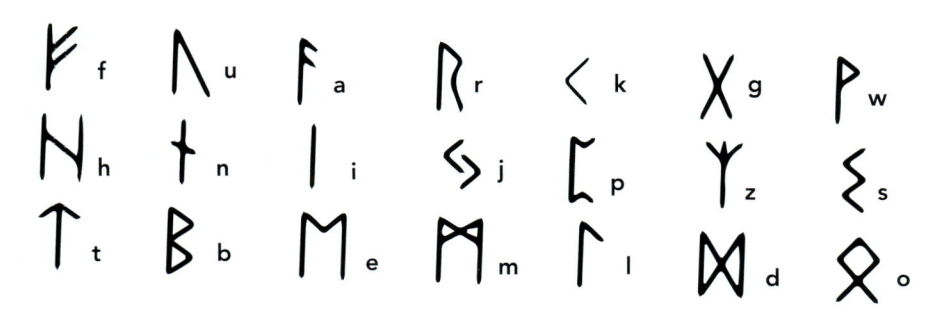

? Quick quiz

1. Which country is named after the Franks?
   a) France
   b) Germany
   c) Ireland

2. Who sacked Rome in 410?
   a) Visigoths
   b) Ostrogoths
   c) Vandals

See pages 132–133 for the answers

Were all Vikings raiders?

From around 790 to 1100, coastal villages from Western to Eastern Europe were subjected to raids from fierce Scandinavian people, called Vikings. They stole things and took people as slaves – but not all Vikings were raiders.

Viking gods
The Vikings had many gods, whom they asked for help in different areas of their lives. Odin was the god of knowledge, Thor was the thunder god, and Freya a goddess of love.

Settlers
Viking ships brought settlers to places as far away as North America. They had to be tough enough to build homes and grow food in distant lands.

Craftspeople
The Vikings wove baskets and carved designs into wood and walrus ivory. Blacksmiths made beautifully patterned metal items.

Farmers
Most Vikings spent more time farming than fighting. They raised cattle, sheep, and goats. They grew oats, rye, and barley.

Traders
Vikings sailed to Eastern Europe to trade iron and other goods for items such as amber. They travelled to the Middle East for silk and spices.

Odin   Thor   Freya

Who were the Normans?

In 911, the French king paid off battling Vikings by granting them a duchy, or area to rule over, in northern France. Their descendants were great castle builders, and invaded lands around the Mediterranean. In 1066, they conquered England, and their leader, William, became king.

Jarl
The first warrior bands were loyal to the local chieftain, called the jarl. Later kingdoms grew up with powerful rulers.

Raiders
Viking raiders fought with axes and swords. They looted coastal villages for valuable items. Later, warrior bands joined together to form big armies.

? Quick quiz

1. Which Norman became King of England in 1066?

2. Who was the Viking god of thunder?

3. What did Viking longboats have on their prows?

See pages 132–133 for the answers

50 THE MIDDLE AGES

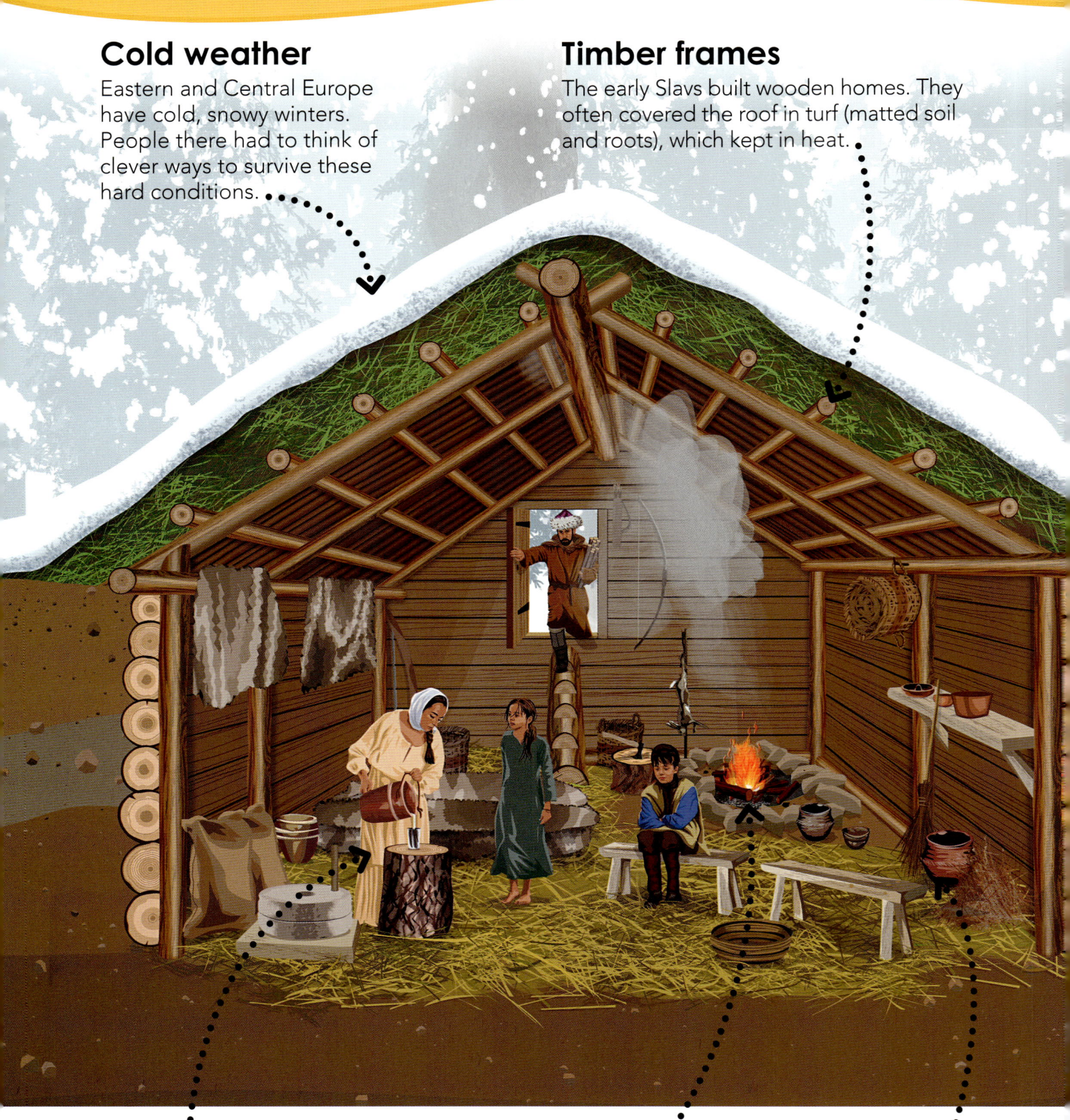

Cold weather
Eastern and Central Europe have cold, snowy winters. People there had to think of clever ways to survive these hard conditions.

Timber frames
The early Slavs built wooden homes. They often covered the roof in turf (matted soil and roots), which kept in heat.

Farming
The plains and river valleys were good for growing wheat and millet. The grains were ground into flour for bread using millstones.

A warm stove
In each hut there was an oven made of clay or stone. Food included hunted boar and farm produce, such as honey.

Craft skills
The early Slavs were skilled at making clay pots. They also carved wooden bowls.

Why did Slavs build sunken homes?

In the 500s CE, Eastern Europe was home to various peoples. The Slavs lived around three big rivers, the upper Vistula, the lower Danube, and the Dnieper. They had clever ways of surviving cold winters, such as by building houses half-sunk into the ground.

In the ground
Packed earth around homes kept out the cold. This type of home was built by some other peoples, too.

What became of the Slavs?

East Slavs
They traded with Swedish Vikings, and their city of Novgorod (pictured) had become a thriving centre by 859. Their descendants are Russians, Belarussians, and Ukrainians.

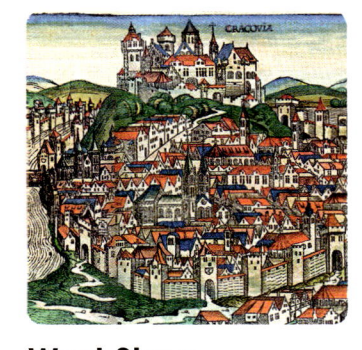

West Slavs
They built great medieval cities, such as Prague and Kraków (above). Their descendants are Czechs, Slovaks, and Poles.

South Slavs
Many Slavs moved into the Balkan lands, such as Serbia and Croatia. Others lived in settlements with Turkic Bulgars, to the west of the Black Sea.

What is the Cyrillic script?
The followers of two Christian saints, Cyril and Methodius, brought new ways of writing the alphabet to the Slavs in the 800s. Today's Russian alphabet is still called Cyrillic.

АБВГДЕЁЖЗИ
A　Be　Ve　Ge　De　Ye　Yo　Zhe　Ze　I

❓ Quick quiz

1. What is the Russian alphabet called?
2. What country is Kraków in today?

See pages 132–133 for the answers

Could anyone become a knight?

From the 11th century, during Europe's Middle Ages, fighting men on horseback became very important people. They were known as knights and they fought in battle for their lord or their king.

Page
Aged seven, a noble boy would be sent to live at another castle. There, he would serve drinks during meals and practise fighting skills.

Noble birth
Most knights were the sons of lords – who were called nobles. A few non-noble fighters might be knighted after a battle.

What was heraldry?
On the battlefield, it was hard to tell who was who beneath their armour, so a family emblem was displayed on shields and tunics. The designs and colours followed a strict set of rules, called heraldry.

Shields of heraldry

Esquire

At 14, the page would become an esquire. This meant following a knight to battle, to help him with his horses, armour, and weapons.

? Quick quiz

1. At what age could a boy become an esquire?

2. What is jousting?

3. What was the name of the knights' code of honour?

See pages 132–133 for the answers

Knight

From around 21, an esquire could become a knight. During a special ceremony, a lord or king would briefly lay a sword on his shoulder, making him a knight.

Landowner

If a knight swore loyalty to his lord, he might be granted land, or even a castle, in return.

What was a tournament?

The first tournaments were violent mock battles, used for training. From the 1200s to the 1500s they became great festivals, with sports such as jousting – where riders tried to dismount each other with lances.

Castles could be attacked by enemy knights, so they had thick walls.

THE MIDDLE AGES

Al-Andalus
Most of Spain and Portugal, and part of France, was conquered by Muslims in the 700s. Architecture and the arts flourished.

The Great Mosque of Córdoba, Spain

Ben Youssef Mosque, Morocco

North Africa
The Maghreb (northwest Africa), home of the Berber people, became a great centre of Islamic learning and of trade across the Sahara Desert.

? Quick quiz

1. What is a caliphate?
2. How long was Ibn Battuta's route?
3. What was the largest caliphate?

See pages 132–133 for the answers

EUROPE

SPAIN
Córdoba

Maghreb

AFRICA

Ibn Battuta's route
Ibn Battuta (1304–1369) went on a great expedition across Muslim lands from Central Asia to Africa and Spain. He travelled 120,000 km (75,000 miles) in total.

How quickly did Islam grow?

After the death of the Muslim prophet Muhammad in 632, Islamic states, called caliphates, grew up in the Middle East, led by religious leaders called caliphs. Within 150 years the powers of these caliphates had spread into Asia, and across North Africa and into Spain.

Umayyad caliphate

From 661–744 the city of Damascus, in Syria, became the centre of a vast empire covering over 11 million sq km (6.8 million sq miles).

Umayyad Mosque, Syria

Harun al-Rashid

Abbasid caliphate

The city of Baghdad, in Iraq, became a centre of science, the arts, and trade. The rule of Harun al-Rashid (786–809) is now called a "golden age".

Baghdad

Damascus

ASIA

How was Islam spread?

Trade and travel
Islam was spread by merchants along trading routes and by seafarers. It was also spread by teachers and missionaries.

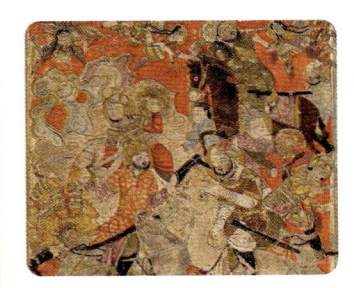

War and conquest
At the battle of Badr in 624 (pictured), Muhammad and his followers defeated the Qureshi of Mecca. Later, wars of conquest spread Islam far beyond Arabia.

Who were the best horse riders in history?

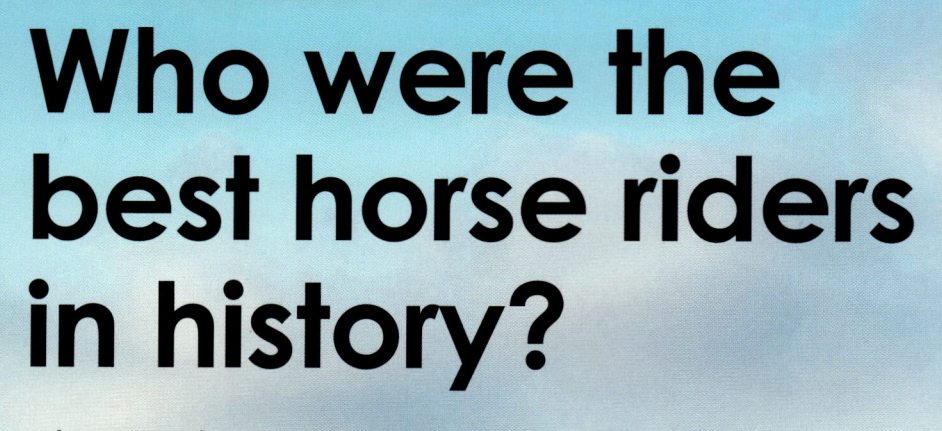

The wide open spaces of steppe grassland and desert in Central Asia were home to nomadic Turkic and Mongol peoples. From the 1200s their tireless horsemen rode into China, Korea, Western Asia, and Eastern Europe to win great empires.

Fluttering flags
Flags with fringes and tails were flown. People also carried banners made of horse or yak hair, called tugs.

Tug

Movable home
A circular tent made of felt was tied over a wooden frame. Called a ger or yurt, it could be packed up and transported on an ox wagon.

Who were the greatest rulers of the steppes?

Genghis Khan
The various Mongol tribes were united by Genghis Khan (c.1162–1227). He then began invading neighbouring lands. His troops were often violent to the people they conquered.

Khubilai Khan
The grandson of Genghis Khan, Khubilai Khan (1215–1294) ruled Mongolia, China, Tibet, and Korea as emperor. He was the founder of the Yuan dynasty in China, and he adopted a Chinese way of life.

Timur
Timur (1370–1405) came from a Turkic tribe with Mongolian ancestors. He wanted to restore Genghis Khan's empire, and he founded the Islamic Timurid Empire. Timur was undefeated in battle.

Expert riders
Warriors had several horses to swap between if one got tired – which meant riding without rest. Stirrups allowed them to use a bow while riding.

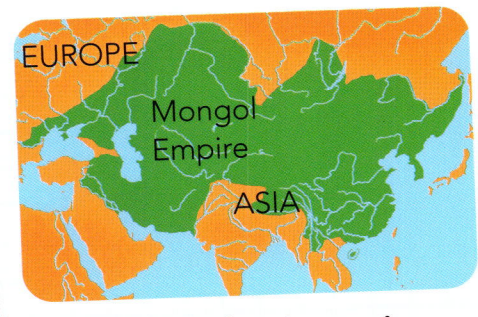

Khubilai Khan's empire

How big was the Mongol Empire?
The empire stretched from the Pacific to Central Europe. It became the biggest joined-up empire in history, at 12 million sq km (7.5 million sq miles).

Quick quiz

1. What is a yurt?
2. What are steppes?
3. Which Mongol khan founded the Yuan dynasty in China?

See pages 132–133 for the answers

What is a Chinese dynasty?

China's long history is divided into dynasties – periods of rule by one royal family. Dynasties could last for hundreds of years before another family took power. Here are some of the most important.

Xia Dynasty
According to legend, the first Chinese dynasty, Xia, was founded by Yu the Great. One story tells of how he saved China from a great flood.

2100–1600 BCE

China's Grand Canal

581–618
Sui Dynasty
Buddhism became more popular in China during this dynasty. A large part of the Grand Canal was built, mainly to transport food.

618–906
Tang Dynasty
This was known as a golden age of poetry, music, painting, and woodblock printing. The Chinese city of Chang'an became the world's biggest city.

Gunpowder, which is used in fireworks, was invented in the Tang Dynasty.

Chinese compass

907–1125
Liao Dynasty
This dynasty did not rule the whole of China, but conquered the northeastern part. It was ruled by the Khitan people.

960–1279
Song Dynasty
Plenty of great art, music, and literature were made during this period, as well as inventions including the bank note. However, there were also many wars.

Who were the "Sons of Heaven"?

The rulers of the Zhou Dynasty, such as King You (pictured), spread the idea that they were chosen by the universe to rule. They called themselves the "Sons of Heaven".

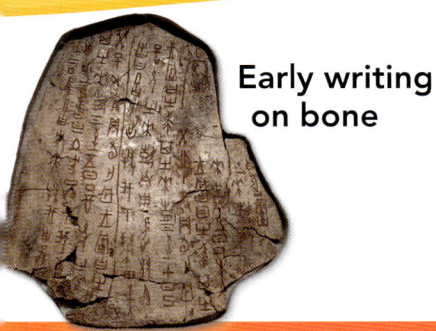

Early writing on bone

Zhou Dynasty
This was China's longest dynasty, though there were wars to try to topple it. New sets of beliefs grew up, such as Confucianism.

How long is the Great Wall of China?
The Great Wall is a series of fortifications, joined up over many centuries. If you add up all the different parts, it comes to 21,196 km (13,170 miles).

1600–1050 BCE

1050–256 BCE

Shang Dynasty
Characters from the modern Chinese system of writing, Hanzi, began to be used during this period.

A Han emperor's court

Qin Dynasty
Qin Shi Huang, the Qin Dynasty's founder, joined the whole of China under one dynasty.

The Great Wall of China

206 BCE–220 CE

221–206 BCE

Han Dynasty
There were wars, rebellions, and invasions from the north during this dynasty – but there were also inventions, such as paper, and plenty of trade.

? Quick quiz

1. In which dynasty were Hanzi characters first used?
2. In which dynasty did China become part of the Mongol Empire?

See pages 132–133 for the answers

Ming dynasty woodblock print

1279–1368

1368–1644

1644–1912

Yuan Dynasty
Under Khubilai Khan, China became part of the huge Mongol Empire. Pottery with blue and red designs became popular.

Ming Dynasty
Chinese rule returned. The country's fleets visited Asia and Africa. From the 1550s, silks and porcelains were traded with Europeans.

Qing Dynasty
From the 1800s, China was invaded by European powers. After wars and rebellions, the last dynasty ended in 1912.

Chinese porcelain

THE MIDDLE AGES

Who were the samurai?

From 1185, the samurai were a class of elite warriors in Japan. They were fierce fighters, who swore loyalty to their feudal lord, or *daimyo*. Their strict code of honour was called *bushido*, which means "the way of the warrior".

Bow and arrows
Samurai were skilled archers. Shooting arrows from horseback was the mark of a good warrior.

Riding
The best samurai could ride a horse into battle while using weapons. The skill of horseback riding was called *bajutsu*.

How powerful were samurai?
Japan had an emperor, but real power was held by warlords, called shoguns. Next in importance were the samurai and their lords. Most Japanese people were peasants who had no power.

Emperor
Shogun
Daimyo
Samurai
Peasants

Samurai

Samurai fought on foot or on horseback. Their weapons included poles with curved blades. From the mid 1500s, some samurai used guns.

How was Himeji Castle protected?

Himeji Castle in Japan was protected by samurai from when it was built in 1333. If attackers made it over the moat, they were faced with arrow fire from unseen warriors. The walls had many small windows, called loopholes, to shoot from.

Armour

Samurai armour was made up of iron and leather plates, tied together and painted with a shiny, see-through coat. Samurai often wore chainmail under their armour.

Sword

Samurai carried a pair of swords. The long sword, or *katana*, and the shorter *wakizashi* were made of the purest steel.

? Quick quiz

1. To whom did a samurai swear loyalty?

2. What were samurai swords made of?

3. Could women be samurai?

See pages 132–133 for the answers

62 THE MIDDLE AGES

Confucianism
The ideas of Confucius began to be followed in Korea during the Joseon Dynasty. He taught about virtue (goodness), the family, morals, and the state.

Confucius was a Chinese philosopher, or thinker.

The design on this Joseon ceramic vase shows a tiger, birds, and hills.

The new sundial's curved shape gave more accurate time than older, fla[t] sundials.

Arts
The people of the Korean peninsula began making pottery thousands of years ago. During the Joseon era, artists became expert at making shiny white ceramics with detailed designs.

Which Korean dynasty lasted 505 years?

The Joseon Dynasty began in 1392 and ruled for 505 years – making it the longest in Korean history. While Joseon rulers fought off invasions, the people invented new things, followed new sets of beliefs, and improved styles of art.

The name Korea comes from Goryeo, or Koryo, a dynasty founded in 918.

Great inventions

Amongst the inventions that came from the Joseon period were a rain gauge, for telling how much rain had fallen, and a better sundial than had existed before.

Fighting invasions

Japanese invaders (below) attacked Korea in the 1590s. Korea was invaded time after time by its neighbours, including the Japanese, Chinese, Mongols, and Russians.

? Quick quiz

1. How did Korea get its name?

2. Which was Korea's longest dynasty?

3. Today Korea is divided into which two countries?

See pages 132–133 for the answers

Where were the three Korean kingdoms?

From 67 BCE to 668 CE, Korea was divided into three main kingdoms. Goguryeo became the largest state. Baekje was in the southwest. In 562 CE, the southeastern kingdom of Silla grew larger by conquering the region of Gaya.

Why was kimchi invented?

Koreans needed to preserve food, or stop it rotting, during winter – when crops wouldn't grow. By 1,500 years ago, they had begun storing salted vegetables in pots underground to make delicious, spicy preserves called kimchi, which are still popular today.

The three kingdoms

THE MIDDLE AGES

Wat Mahathat
This Buddhist temple was built by a ruler of the Kingdom of Ayutthaya, which was founded in 1351.

Wat Lokayasutharam
Another wonder of the Ayutthaya Kingdom, this monastery has a 40-m- (130-ft-) long statue of the Buddha lying down.

Borobudur
This massive Buddhist temple is on the island of Java, Indonesia. It was built around 800 CE by the rulers of the Mataram Kingdom.

Angkor Wat
This Hindu (later, Buddhist) temple is the world's largest religious site. It was built between 1122–1150 for the Khmer rulers of Cambodia.

Thailand

Cambodia

JAVA SEA

Indonesia

Java

Who built temples in Southeast Asia?

Many magnificent religious monuments survive amidst the tropical forests and rice fields of Southeast Asia, and on its volcanic islands. They were built by powerful kingdoms from the 800s to the 1500s.

Which kings fought one another on elephant-back?

Wars between the kings of Ayutthaya and the Burmese Toungoo Empire broke out from 1547. During one battle in 1593, the Thai King Naresuan and the Burmese Prince Mingyi Swa fought each other on elephants.

What was the largest sea-based empire in Southeast Asia?

The Majapahit Hindu-Buddhist Empire was centred on Java, but conquered lands all around the Java Sea. It reached the height of its power in 1350–1389. Art and writing flourished in the empire.

Bajang Ratu arch, Trowulan, Java

? Quick quiz

1. The Khmer civilization grew up in which modern country?

2. Which religions were followed at Angkor Wat?

3. Who brought Islam to the islands?

See pages 132–132 for the answers

How rich was Mansa Musa?

Some say Musa was the richest man ever. In 1324 he left his home of Mali, in western Africa, for a pilgrimage to Mecca. His procession included thousands of men, elephants, and camels weighed down with gold.

King of Mali
Musa was Mansa (ruler) of the Muslim empire of Mali. He took over the city of Timbuktu and turned it into a centre of learning and trade.

Who else flourished in Mali's time?

Songhai Empire
The Songhai people founded a state south of the Sahara. They lost Gao (left) and Timbuktu to Mali, but later won back the cities. They ran a Muslim empire larger than Mali between c.1464–1591.

Benin
This kingdom (1180–1897) was founded by the Edo people in the forests of what is now southwestern Nigeria. It was famous for its city walls, and its fine heads and statues made of bronze and brass (left).

Hausa states
Between c.1000 and 1815, seven Hausa kingdoms, now in northern Nigeria, traded in indigo-dyed cloth (left), hides, leather, salt, kola nuts, and gold. They became Muslim in the 1300s and 1400s.

How were the Benin bronzes made?

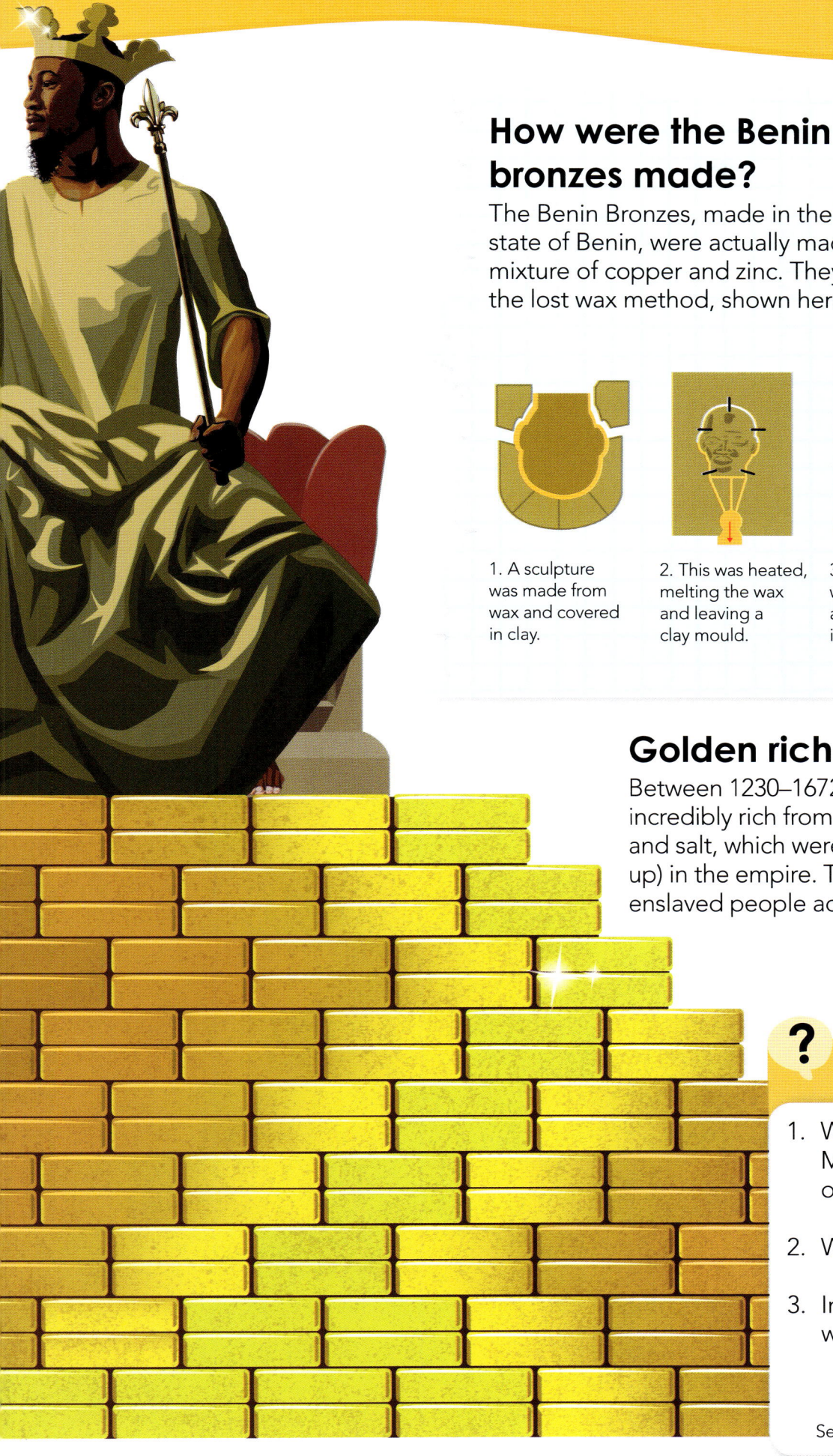

The Benin Bronzes, made in the West African state of Benin, were actually made from brass – a mixture of copper and zinc. They were cast using the lost wax method, shown here.

1. A sculpture was made from wax and covered in clay.

2. This was heated, melting the wax and leaving a clay mould.

3. The metal was melted and poured into the mould.

4. The metal cooled and hardened, and the clay was broken off.

Golden riches

Between 1230–1672 Mali grew incredibly rich from trading gold and salt, which were mined (dug up) in the empire. They also traded enslaved people across the Sahara.

? Quick quiz

1. Which city did Mansa Musa turn into a centre of learning?

2. What does Mansa mean?

3. In which modern country was the Benin Kingdom?

See pages 132–133 for the answers

How did Zimbabwe get its name?

This country is named after Great Zimbabwe – a ruined, royal capital built by ancestors of the Shona people, who live in Zimbabwe today. "Zimbabwe" comes from "dzimba-dza-mabwe", or "houses of stone" in the Shona language.

Great Zimbabwe

This site covers over 7 sq km (4.3 sq miles). Different parts of it were built at different times. People lived there from around 1100–1450.

Where did Bantu people migrate?

The Shona are part of the Bantu group of people. Between c.1500 BCE–1500 CE, Bantu peoples migrated from West Africa to East, South, and Central Africa, bringing farming and metalworking skills.

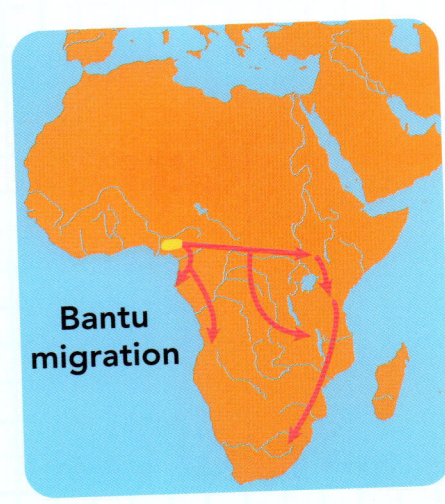

Bantu migration

How did the Swahili culture form?

Bantu peoples along the East African coast formed their own language and culture during the Middle Ages, partly inspired by the Arabs and Persians they traded with. This was the Swahili culture.

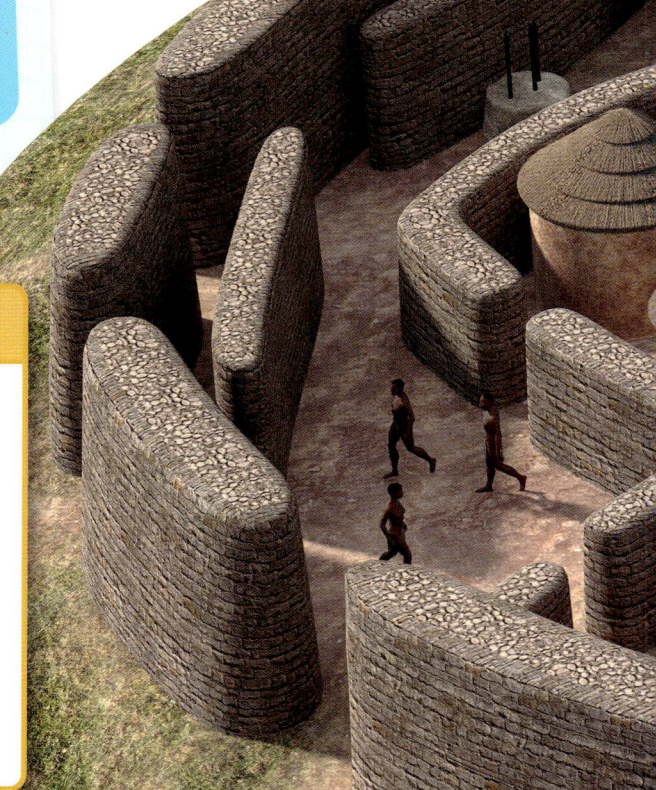

Outer walls

These granite walls surround an inner wall built much earlier. They are 11 m (37 ft) high and 6 m (20 ft) thick in places.

Clay house

Inside the walls, some houses were built with earth and mud-bricks. The whole site was probably home to over 10,000 people.

? Picture quiz

The national emblem of Zimbabwe is based on sculptures found at Great Zimbabwe. What is it?

See pages 132–133 for the answers

Who are the Indigenous Peoples of North America?

The people who have lived in North America since before the arrival of Europeans are called Indigenous. There are many different peoples, speaking more than 150 languages, and each has their own traditional way of life.

What is the oldest sport still played in North America?

Lacrosse is a game with netted sticks and a rubber ball. It was already being played in the 1100s. The original version was very violent, with hundreds of people joining in!

Haida apron

Northwest
People on the northwest coasts once survived by fishing and whaling. They carved cedarwood and painted different styles of art.

Pueblo cliff dwellings

Southwest
The Pueblo peoples were farmers, potters, and weavers. Mesa Verde's cliff dwellings date from the 1190s.

? Quick quiz

1. Is Greenland part of North America?
2. Did the Indigenous Peoples ride horses?
3. Where do Haida people come from?

See pages 132–133 for the answers

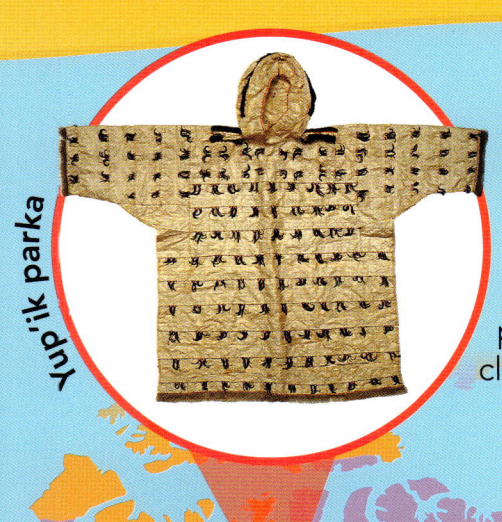

Arctic

Arctic peoples include communities of Inuit and Yup'ik. Traditionally, they hunted walruses, seals, and polar bears, and made warm clothes of fur and hide.

Yup'ik parka

Subarctic

Below the Arctic sit great northern forests. People there once survived by fishing and hunting caribou and moose. They used snowshoes and toboggans.

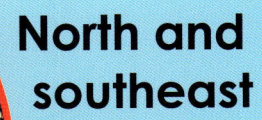

Cree Canoe

North and southeast

For hundreds of years, maize, squash, and beans were grown here in farming villages, such as the Powhatan village of Secotan.

Powhatan village

Plains

The prairies were once used for farming and buffalo hunting. Europeans brought horses, which Indigenous Peoples used for hunting.

Tipi

Arctic
Subarctic
Great Basin
Plains
Northeast
Southeast
Southwest

THE MIDDLE AGES

Which Aztec city was in the middle of a lake?

In c.1325, the Aztecs founded the city of Tenochtitlan on a little island in Lake Texcoco, in what is now Mexico City. They built temples and squares, which soon filled with people. The city eventually had a population of over 250,000.

Chinampas
The Aztecs built up patches of land from the lake bed to grow crops. They used poles, reed fences, mud, and willow roots to bind the soil.

Who were the Aztec gods?
The Aztecs made offerings to their many gods, whom they believed looked after them. They sacrificed humans to sustain their gods.

Huitzilopochtli

Eagles and Jaguars
These two military academies provided elite troops. They fought with bows and arrows, clubs, spears, and darts. The Eagles wore feathers and the Jaguars wore spotted animal skins.

Who conquered the Aztecs?

From 1519 to 1521, Spanish soldiers led by Hernán Cortés (pictured) defeated the Aztec Empire. Portuguese and Spanish "Conquistadors", such as these, overran the Americas. They were violent and greedy for gold – and they brought diseases.

? Quick quiz

1. What modern city is on the site of Tenochtitlan?
2. Which animals were Aztec soldiers named after?
3. Did Aztecs place bets on the ball games?

See pages 132–133 for the answers

Great temple

Aztecs built pyramids topped with two temples, one for Tlaloc and the other for Huitzilopochtli. These gods were very important to the Aztecs.

Food and drink

The Aztec diet included beans, squash, chili peppers, tortillas, tomatoes, sweet potatoes, maize, avocadoes, fish, turkey, duck eggs, and a frothy drink made from chocolate.

Sport

The Aztecs played a game with teams and a rubber ball that they bounced off their bodies. The court had sloping sides to run up.

Who built Machu Picchu?

The Incas built this mountain-top site in the 1400s, for their emperor Pachacuti. His empire lay between the Andes mountains and the Pacific Ocean, with Cusco, in modern Peru, as its capital. The Inca civilization lasted from the 1200s to the 1500s.

Machu Picchu
The town included houses, workshops for making crafts, temples, and water channels. It was home to up to 1,000 people.

Earthquake-proof architecture
The Incas were precise builders, with close-fitting stones that would stay in place even during an earthquake.

Did the Incas have computers?

No – but they had devices to store data, like a computer. The quipu was a bundle of cords, often colour-coded, which was used to record numbers. It was knotted to show taxes, and helped officials run the empire.

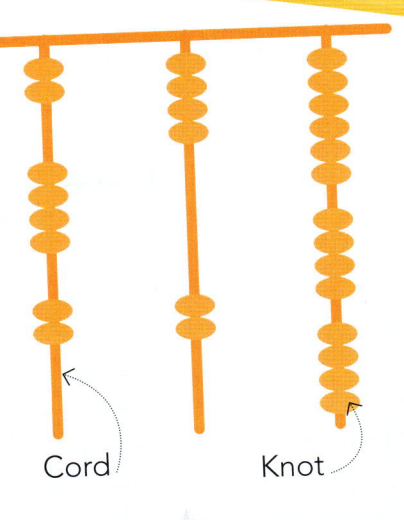

Cord
Knot

How did the Incas get things up a mountain?

The Incas had no strong animals, such as horses, to pull wheeled carts. Instead, they used llamas to carry packs along mountain roads and over rope bridges. Llamas and alpacas also provided wool for clothing.

Terraces

To farm on steep mountainsides, the Incas built narrow fields as terraces (giant steps). Inca crops included potatoes and maize.

? True or false?

1. Machu Picchu was the capital of Pachacuti's empire.

2. The Incas used horses to carry loads.

3. The Incas used rope bridges.

See pages 132–133 for the answers

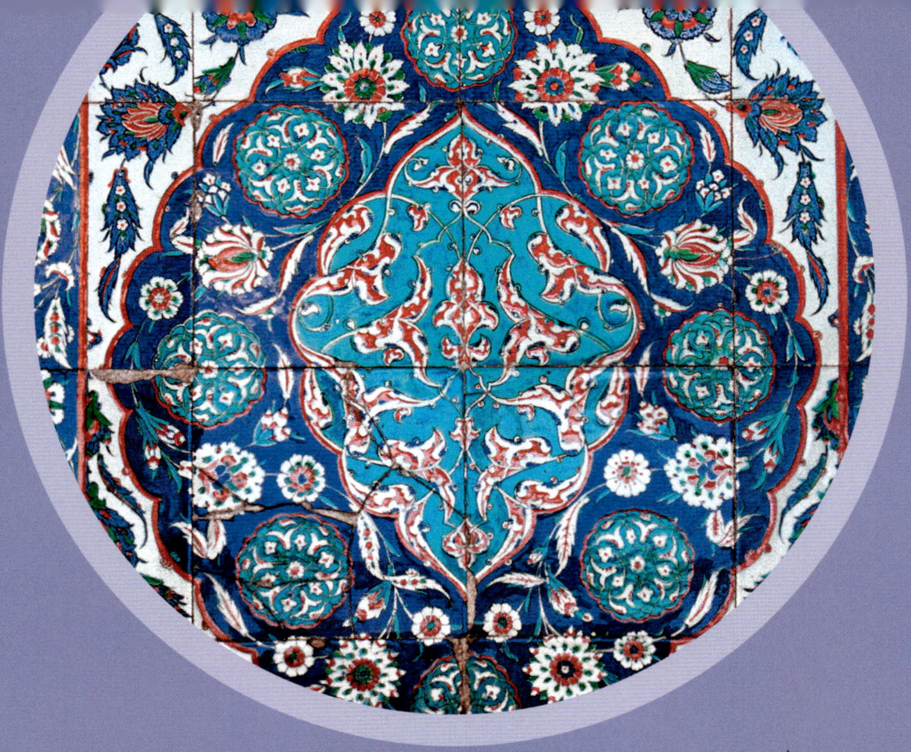

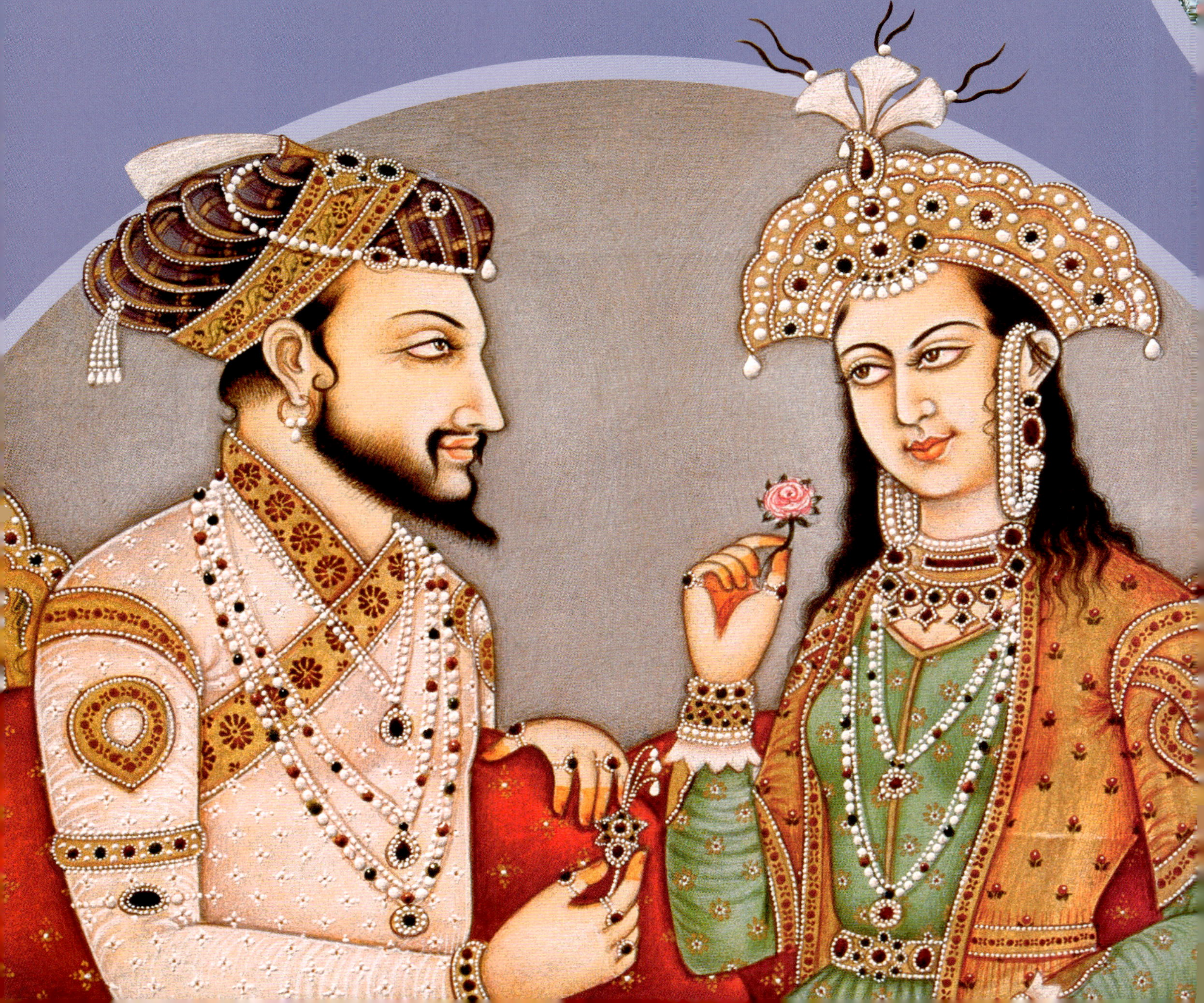

The exploration age

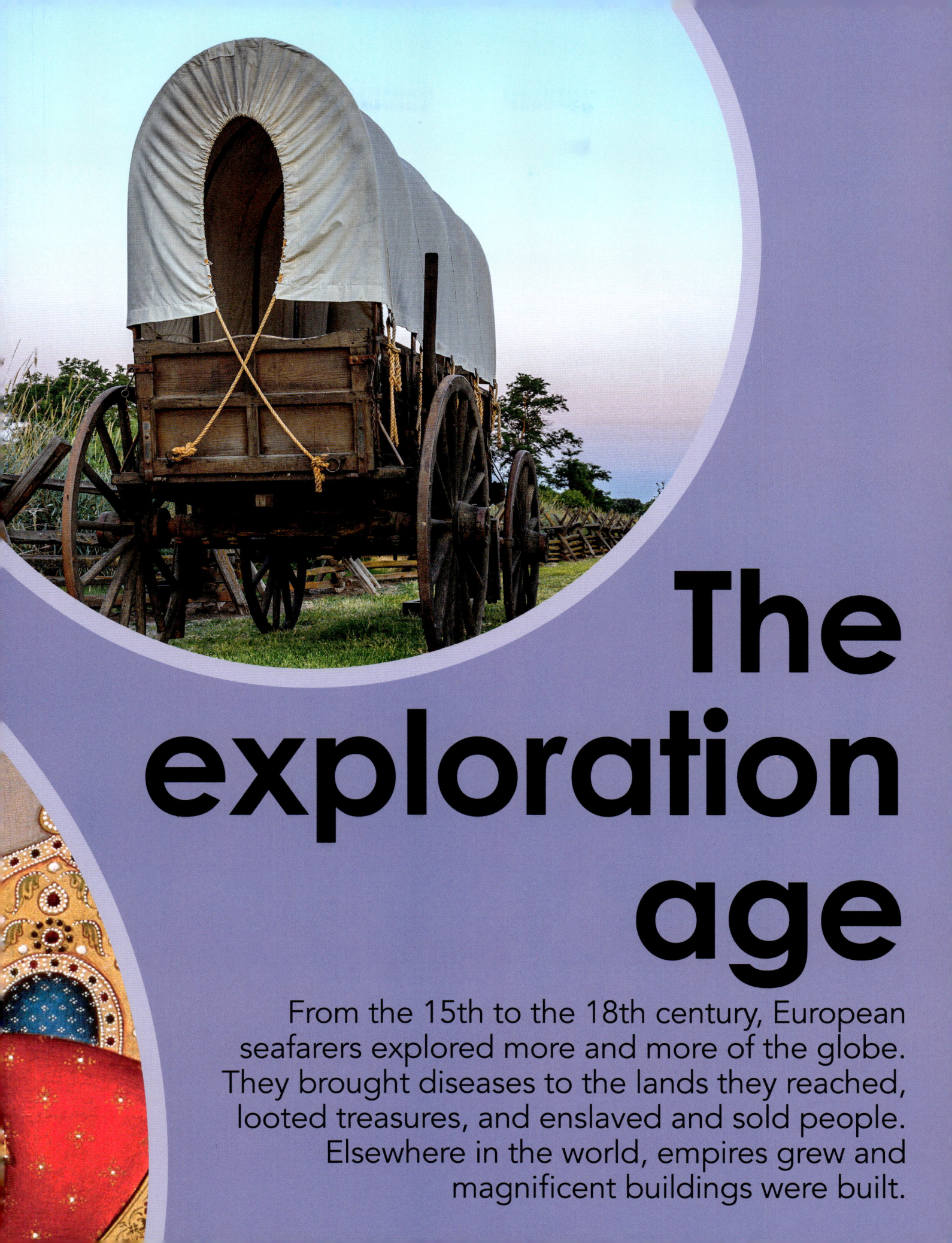

From the 15th to the 18th century, European seafarers explored more and more of the globe. They brought diseases to the lands they reached, looted treasures, and enslaved and sold people. Elsewhere in the world, empires grew and magnificent buildings were built.

THE EXPLORATION AGE

How can you spot Renaissance architecture?
Like Roman and Greek buildings, Renaissance palaces and churches have columns supporting pediments, arches, and domes. Florence Cathedral's magnificent dome (pictured) was made with 4 million bricks.

Arch  Column Dome Pediment

Inventing
Inventions during the Renaissance included the microscope and the telescope, for seeing things close up and far away. Leonardo's ideas for new technology included a flying machine.

Leonardo's plans for a flying machine

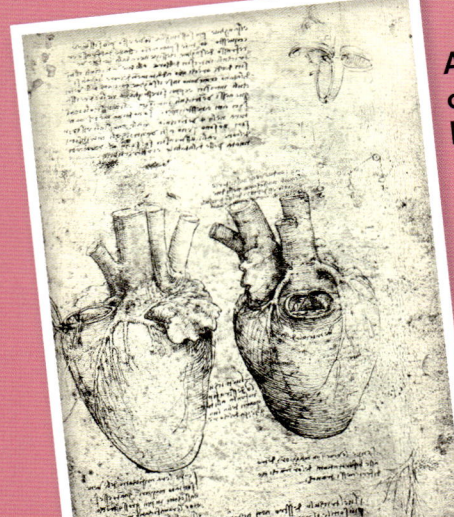

A drawing of a heart by Leonardo

Science
Renaissance scientists were fascinated by space and by the human body. Leonardo worked out that the heart is a muscle with four chambers, which pumps blood around the body.

Was there anything Da Vinci couldn't do?

Leonardo da Vinci (1452–1519) was a brilliant artist, sculptor, engineer, scientist, and architect – and a lot more besides. He lived in Italy at the end of the Middle Ages during a time famous for its artistic and scientific changes, called the Renaissance.

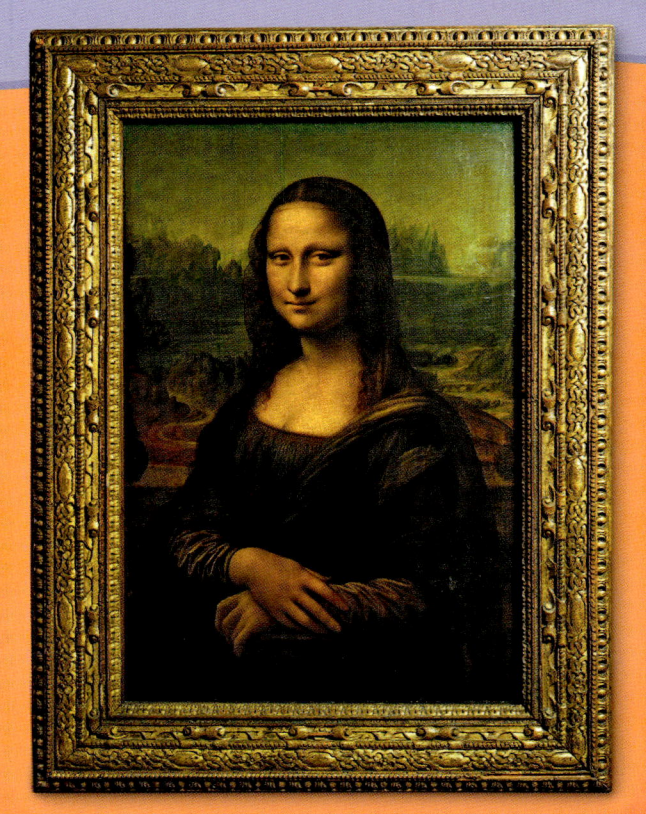

Painting
For Leonardo's *Mona Lisa* portrait, he used newly invented oil paints. He painted dramatic areas of light and shade, and made shadows soft and blurry.

What sort of thing did Renaissance artists paint?

Religion
Artists made Christian art livelier and more realistic. *The Procession of the Magi*, by Italian artist Benozzo Gozzoli (1421–1497), shows three kings from the Bible amongst the splendour of a Renaissance parade.

Nature
People and the natural world were painted in great detail. *Spring* by Italian artist Sandro Botticelli (1445–1510) shows figures from Roman myths, and celebrates the joys of spring.

One of Leonardo's building designs

Architecture
Renaissance buildings swapped out soaring medieval stonework for ancient Greek and Roman features. Leonardo made detailed plans for buildings in this style, but they were never made.

Renaissance figure
The word "renaissance" means "rebirth" in French. People use this word to describe Leonardo's time because of the new art and ideas that appeared, inspired by ancient Greece and Rome.

? Quick quiz

1. What does the word "renaissance" mean?
2. How many bricks are in the great dome of Florence Cathedral?
3. Where can you see the *Mona Lisa* now?

See pages 132–133 for the answers

THE EXPLORATION AGE

When was Europe's age of exploration?

Although Vikings reached North America about 1,000 years ago, Europe's greatest age of exploration was from the 1400s. People sailed in search of things to trade and people to trade with, or lands to colonize. Mapmakers, scientists, and others followed.

? Quick quiz

1. Who were the first Europeans known to have reached the Americas?
2. Who was Christopher Columbus working for?
3. How long did the first trip around the world take?

See pages 132–133 for the answers

Christopher Columbus
In 1492, this Italian seafarer reached the Caribbean islands – which no one in Europe knew existed. Europeans returned to land on the mainlands of the Americas.

The Bahamas

THE AMERICAS

THE PACIFIC

How did explorers find their way?
The Sun, Moon, and stars appear in different parts of the sky according to where you are on Earth. Sailors used their positions to tell where they were.

An astrolabe shows the angle between the Sun or stars and Earth's surface.

What happened after Europeans explored?

Europe became rich
Spain and Portugal made a fortune by trading what they found, or stole, on their expeditions – followed by England, France, and the Netherlands. More pirates began to sail the seas, looking to loot treasure ships.

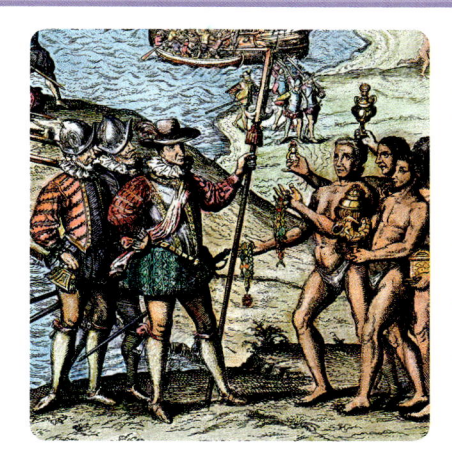

Indigenous Peoples suffered
Many people lost control of their lands and trade. Millions were enslaved, murdered, or given diseases by Europeans. Europe ruled overseas empires for the next 450 years.

Vasco da Gama
In 1498, this Portuguese explorer reached India by sailing around the Cape of Good Hope, South Africa. Portugal now controlled the spice trade, but also engaged in brutal piracy.

Ferdinand Magellan
In 1519, this Portuguese explorer led a Spanish fleet around South America to the Pacific. He was killed in the Philippines and only one ship made it home, in 1522 – the first to sail around the world.

THE EXPLORATION AGE

When did Europeans arrive in North America?

French, English, Dutch, Spanish, and other Europeans all came to colonize (take over) parts of North America between the 1500s and the 1800s. Enslaved people also settled in the American colonies.

Puritans
English Christians seeking religious freedom landed near Cape Cod, Massachusetts, in 1620.

What was the Trail of Tears?

Between 1830 and 1850, the USA forced thousands of Indigenous Peoples – Cherokee, Choctaw, Seminole, Muscogee, and Chickasaw – to leave their eastern homelands and move west of the Mississippi river. Many starved or died of disease along the way.

How did the settlers take over the land?

After 13 English colonies won independence in 1776, the USA bought up new territory, or fought to take it from other Europeans or Indigenous Peoples.

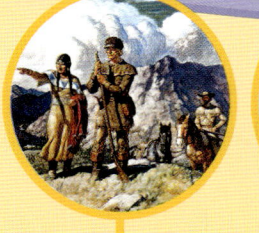

1609–1924
Wars with Indigenous Peoples
Wars often broke out when Europeans or the US government wanted to take over Indigenous lands.

1804–1806
Lewis and Clark expedition
Meriwether Lewis and William Clark were the first US citizens to explore lands westwards to the Pacific coast.

1840s–1860s
The Oregon Trail
US settlers headed west from the Missouri river in covered wagons, on a 3,490-km (2,168-mile) journey to the west coast.

1869
Railways
Train travel linked up the east and west coasts in the USA (1869) and Canada (1885). Now, people could easily move to new places.

Wild landscape
European settlers had to start from scratch to grow food and build homes. They survived with the help of Indigenous Peoples.

Quick quiz

1. When did Puritans arrive in Massachusetts?
2. Which Dutch settlement became New York City?

See pages 132–133 for the answers

Which sultan became The Magnificent?

Süleyman I ruled the Turkish Ottoman Empire from 1520–1566. He was famed and feared in Western Europe, where they called him "the Magnificent" – because of the many battles he waged, and often won.

Taking the seas
The Ottomans attacked the Greek island of Rhodes in 1480 (above) and took the island in 1522. But they lost a major sea battle off Lepanto in 1571.

On to Hungary
The Ottomans advanced westward after capturing Constantinople in 1453. In 1526, Süleyman defeated Hungary at the town of Mohács.

How can you spot Ottoman art?

Ottoman workshops produced magnificent textiles, carpets, pottery, metalwork, and wood inlaid with ivory. Ottoman artists loved patterns of flowers, especially tulips and carnations, as well as fruit and vines.

? Quick quiz

1. What is a Sultan?
2. For how long did the Ottomans control the Middle East?
3. Did Süleyman I win control over Austria?

See pages 132–133 for the answers

Laying siege to Vienna

In 1529, Süleyman besieged the Austrian capital, Vienna (above) – which means his army surrounded it and kept on attacking. But they could not capture the city. A second siege, in 1683, also failed.

Capturing Baghdad

In 1534, Süleyman captured Baghdad, in Iraq. This began the Ottoman control of the Middle East, which lasted until 1918.

Who built the Taj Mahal?

Some say that this is the most beautiful building in the world. It was built between 1631–1653 in Agra, India, by the Mughal emperor Shah Jahan. It was a memorial to his beloved wife Mumtaz Mahal – and they are both buried there.

Dome
The biggest dome is 73 m (240 ft) high. It is an onion dome, which means it is pointed at the top – like many other Mughal domes.

Shah Jahan and Mumtaz

Who were the Mughals?

India's Mughal dynasty was founded in 1526 by Babur, an invader from Central Asia. The empire thrived in the 1500s and 1600s under rulers including Akbar and Shah Jahan.

White marble
Mughal buildings were often built using this white stone. It can seem rosy pink at dawn, dazzle in bright sunshine, or reflect soft moonlight by night.

Decoration
The marble is inlaid with stones such as jade, turquoise, jasper, amethyst, and crystal. It shows floral patterns and beautiful lettering.

Arch
A graceful, pointed arch, such as this one, is a clue that shows you might be looking at an Islamic monument.

? True or false?

1. It took 22,000 labourers to build the Taj Mahal.

2. The Mughal empire was founded by a descendent of Timur.

3. Shah Jahan and Mumtaz Mahal are not buried at this site.

See pages 132–133 for the answers

How big was the Mughal Empire?
At its largest, the empire covered more than 4 million sq km (2.5 million sq miles), from what is now Afghanistan to south India. In the 1700s the Mughal Empire began to lose power.

Afghanistan

MUGHAL EMPIRE

India

How did the First Australians live off the land?

People have lived in Australia for about 60,000 years. Over the ages, the First Australians became experts at survival in harsh landscapes, and in conserving (protecting) scarce resources.

Fire
Bushfires are common in Australia. People learned how to make careful use of fire in order to clear land for settlements or to hunt, without destroying whole habitats.

First Australians discovered that certain frogs could be squeezed to provide water.

Water
In dry landscapes, people learned ways to collect water, and the spots where water might naturally pool – such as in rock basins. Plants and mosses might contain water, too.

Hunting
Some people hunted with a boomerang (pictured), fished, and gathered nuts and fruit. Overhunting was avoided, so that animals did not die out, and food was shared.

What is the Dreaming?

The First Australians developed many myths about creation, ancestral beings, sacred landscapes, birds, and animals – some of which are shown in paintings. Such beliefs have been called "the Dreaming", but various words are used to describe them in First Australian languages.

Farming
People planted seeds and irrigated (supplied water to) crops. They grew food such as bush tomatoes, millet, and yams, like the one in this ancient cave painting.

Birds
Certain birds were known to be expert water finders. These birds could be followed to life-giving water even in the desert.

❓ Quick quiz

1. When did people first arrive in Australia?

2. What were boomerangs used for?

3. When did Europeans begin to settle in Australia?

See pages 132–133 for the answers

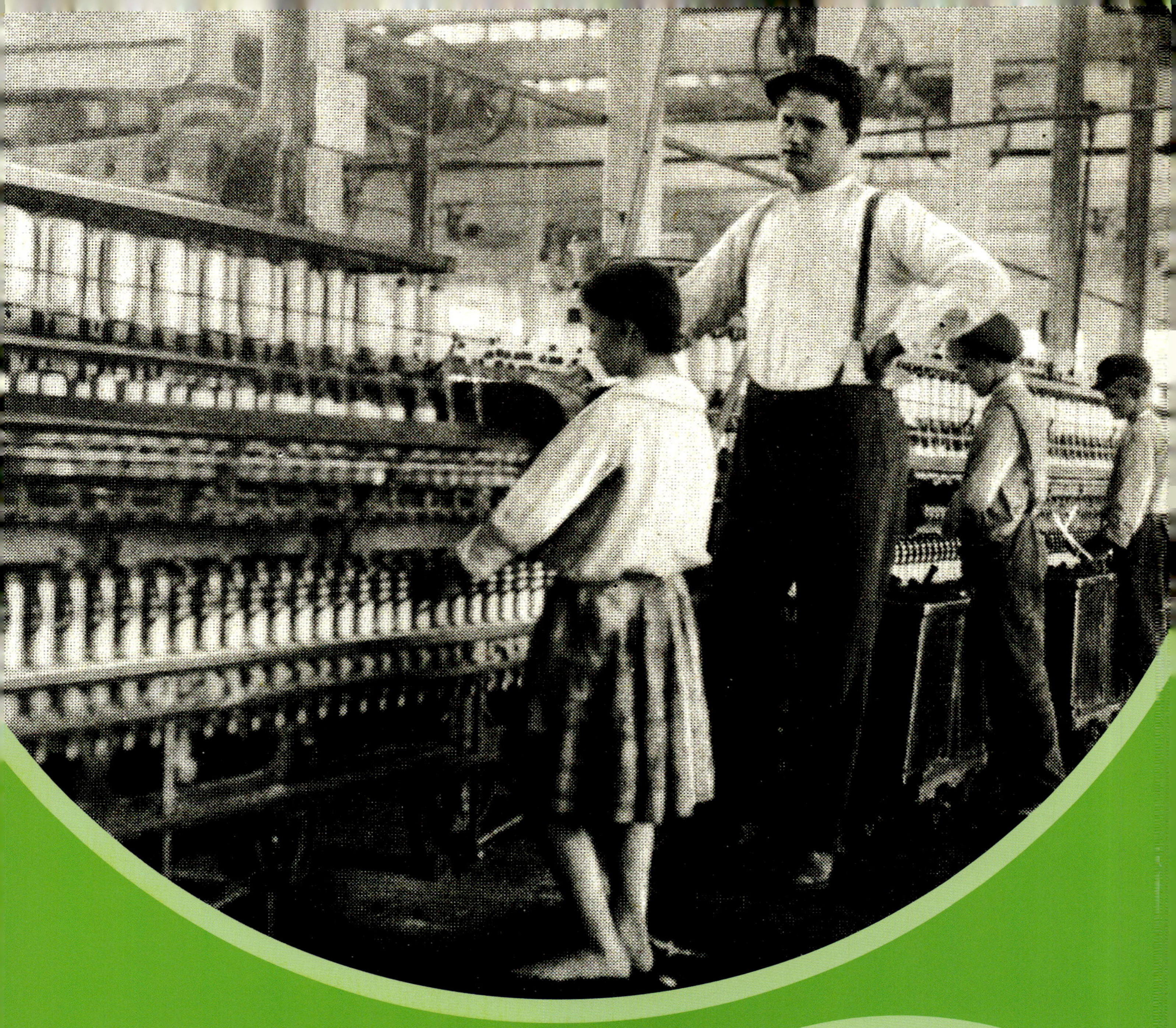
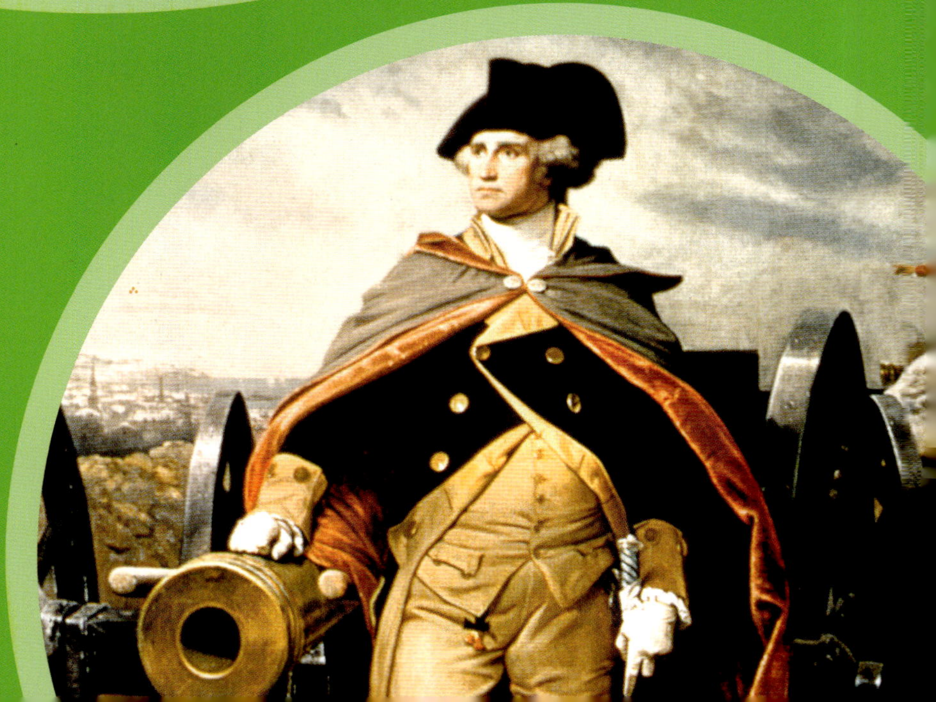

Empires and revolutions

Europe's empires competed to control the world through the 18th and 19th centuries. Governments showed little care for people in overseas colonies, or at home in crowded, dirty cities, and protests grew into revolutions.

How was the USA created?

Up until 1773, 13 of the European colonies in what is now the USA were ruled by Britain. These had to pay taxes to the British government. But why should they give money to a far-away ruler?

Protests
A tax on tea imports angered a group of colonists in Boston. In 1773, they boarded three British ships and threw tea overboard. There had been protests against British rule before – but never this big.

An important meeting
The British closed Boston Harbour and brought in harsh new laws. In 1774, all but one of the colonies founded a rebel government, called the Continental Congress.

War breaks out
In 1775, fighting broke out between rebellious colonists and British soldiers at Lexington. The Congress, now with all 13 colonies, raised an army, and war began. France supported the Congress from 1776.

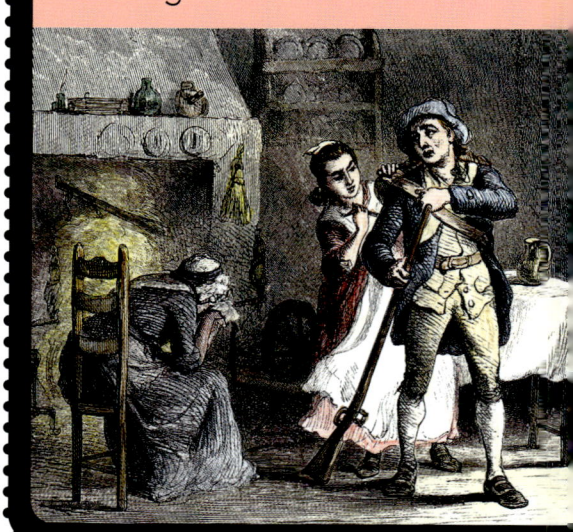

Who was George Washington?
George Washington (1732–1799) was born in the colony of Virginia. He commanded the Continental Army in the American Revolutionary War of 1775–1783, and became the first President of the United States of America in 1789.

Quick quiz

1. When was the Boston Tea Party?
2. Why is 4th July celebrated in the USA?
3. Which agreement ended the war?

See pages 132–133 for the answers

The war is won

In 1781, the British commander Charles Cornwallis surrendered at Yorktown. He asked General Charles O'Hara to hand his sword to Continental Army general Benjamin Lincoln. The war was ended. In the Treaty of Paris of 1783, the British agreed that the USA was its own country.

Declaring independence

The Congress stated their reasons for war in a Declaration of Independence signed on 4 July 1776. They wanted to end the "destructive" rule of the British government over the colonies.

Why did French people rise up in 1789?

Poor people were going hungry and those in charge were not helping them. France was ruled by a king and the Catholic church had too much power. The king grew unpopular and a revolution began.

The women's march
By October of 1789, the market women of Paris, France's capital, had suffered enough. Over 7,000 women marched to the palace at Versailles to demand change.

The French Revolution
The revolution grew more bloody as it went on. Many people thought to be enemies of the revolution, such as nobles, were killed.

14 July 1789
Fall of the Bastille
On 14 July, this fortress prison in Paris was stormed by an angry mob. The revolution had begun.

Who was Napoleon Bonaparte?

Napoleon rose to fame after fighting in the Revolutionary Wars between France and other European countries. He became very powerful, and declared himself Emperor in 1804. Napoleon won battles across Europe, but was defeated at Waterloo, Belgium, in 1815.

? Quick quiz

1. Why is France's national day 14 July?

2. What was the name of Louis XVI's queen?

3. What colours make up the French flag, introduced in 1794?

See pages 132–133 for the answers

To Versailles!

King Louis XVI was forced to leave his palace and go to Paris. In 1793 Louis XVI and his queen, Marie Antoinette, were executed.

1792
The First Republic
The king was overthrown and a Convention was voted in to govern France.

1793–1794
The Reign of Terror
During this violent period, the king, queen, and many others were beheaded by guillotine (pictured).

1795–1799
The Directory
A five-member committee tried to restore law and order. It was overthrown by Napoleon Bonaparte.

What was the Underground Railroad?

No trains travelled on the Underground Railroad. In fact, it wasn't a railway, nor underground. It was a secret network of routes, used from c.1810–1850, by groups of enslaved people in the USA to escape from states where slavery was legal.

About 10.7 million enslaved people were forced to work in the Americas between 1525 and 1866.

Passengers
Many people using the network were born to enslaved parents, and had never been free. Those caught fleeing were sent back and punished harshly.

What was the Atlantic Slave Trade?

From the 1500s, Europeans kidnapped West Africans and took them to the Americas. There, they were sold and forced to do unpaid work, such as growing crops. The trade was outlawed by the early 1800s, but slavery in the USA continued until 1866.

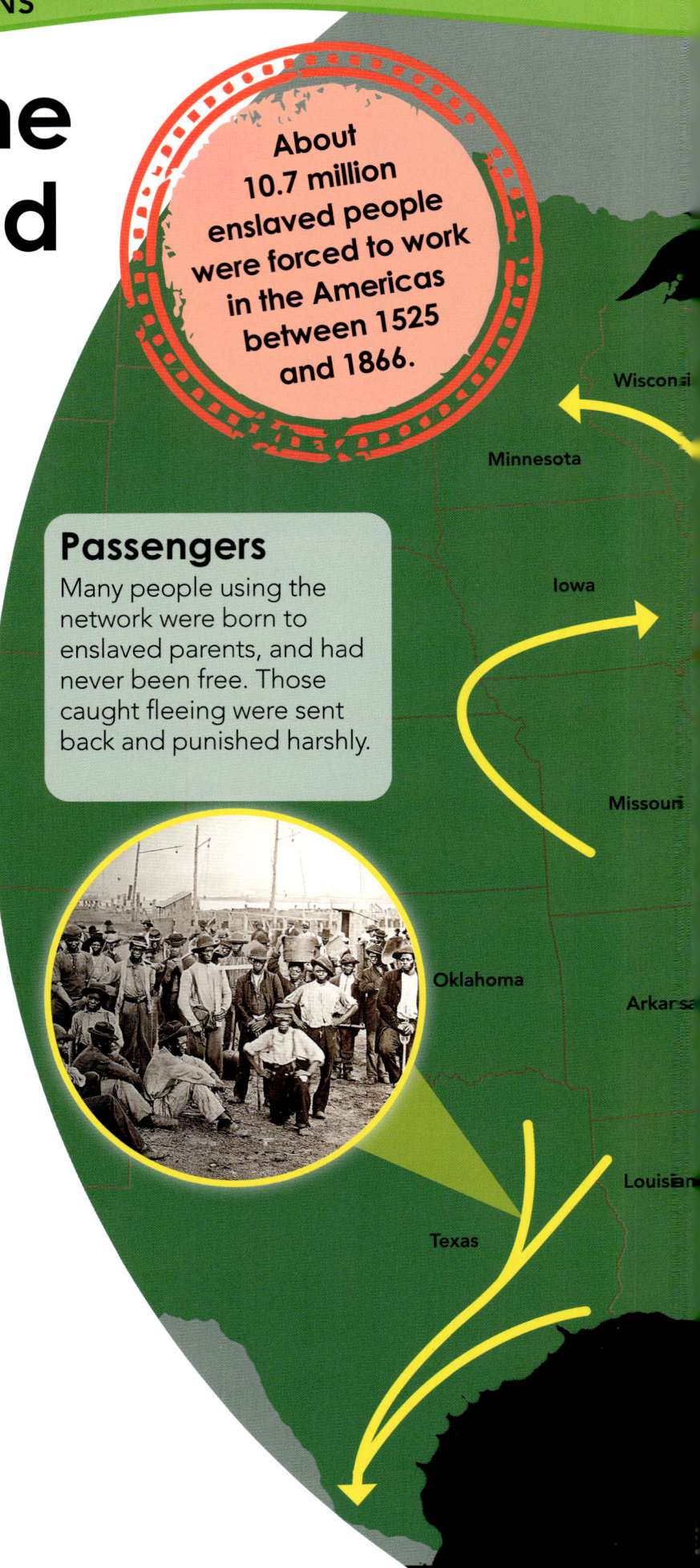

Stations

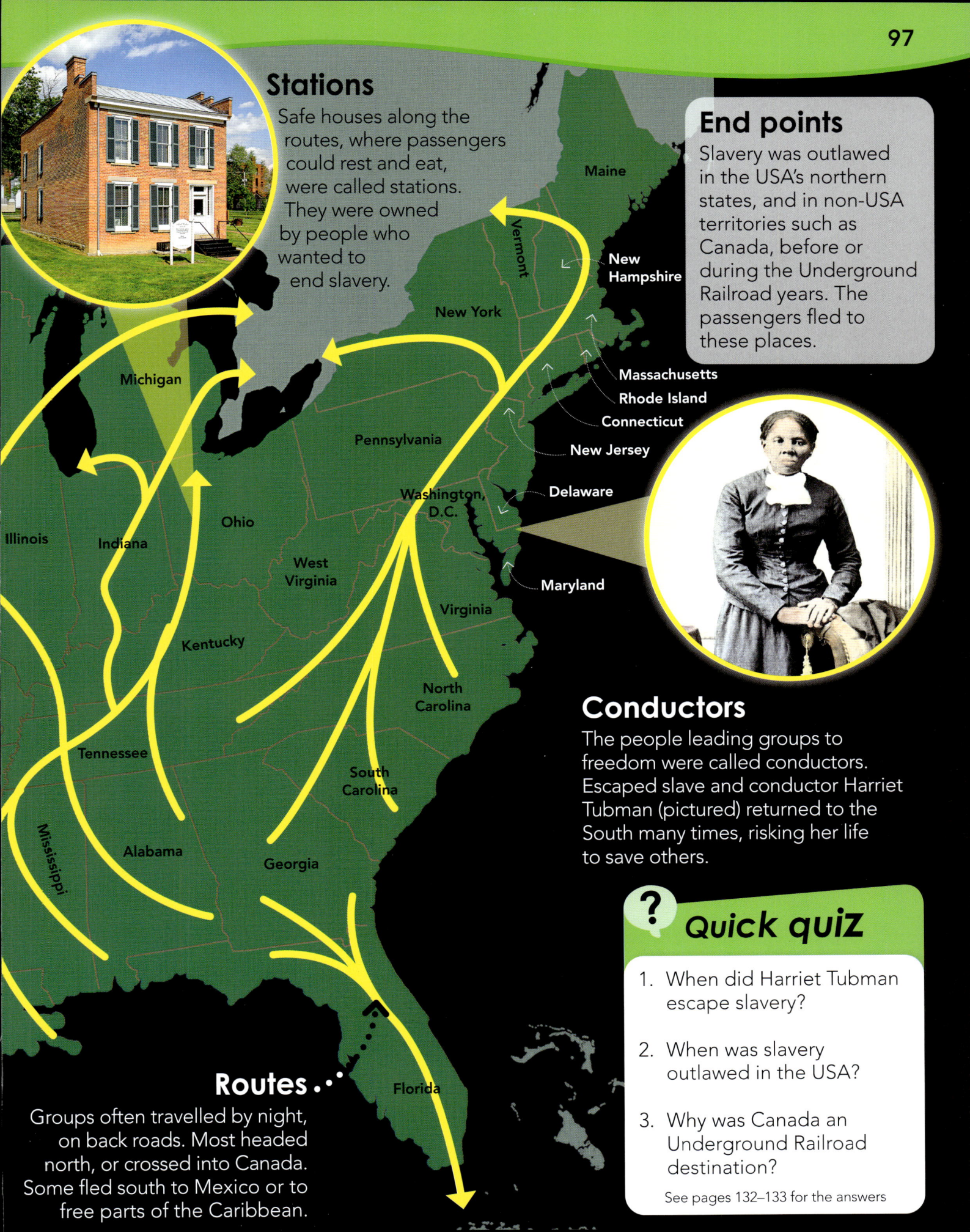

Safe houses along the routes, where passengers could rest and eat, were called stations. They were owned by people who wanted to end slavery.

End points

Slavery was outlawed in the USA's northern states, and in non-USA territories such as Canada, before or during the Underground Railroad years. The passengers fled to these places.

Conductors

The people leading groups to freedom were called conductors. Escaped slave and conductor Harriet Tubman (pictured) returned to the South many times, risking her life to save others.

Routes

Groups often travelled by night, on back roads. Most headed north, or crossed into Canada. Some fled south to Mexico or to free parts of the Caribbean.

? Quick quiz

1. When did Harriet Tubman escape slavery?

2. When was slavery outlawed in the USA?

3. Why was Canada an Underground Railroad destination?

See pages 132–133 for the answers

What work did children once do?

The move from agriculture to industry in the mid-18th century saw the employment of many children in factories and mines across Europe and the USA. Children could be paid less than adults, and were small enough to fit in the narrow gaps behind machinery.

A dirty business
Industrialization meant more factories, which meant more air pollution from the coal – and later gas and oil – burnt to power machinery. More people also moved to cities, looking for work, and these became dirty, overcrowded, and unhealthy places to live.

Cotton mill
Children as young as five worked in textile mills in the USA. They worked around 10–14 hours a day, and did not go to school.

Why did children work in mines?
Children were small enough to crawl along the dark, narrow tunnels of coal mines deep underground. They opened trap doors to let air into the mine, and picked out coals at the pit mouth. Older children pulled trucks of coal along rails.

Overseer
Factory managers were employed to oversee the workers. They often punished the children if they were late or seen talking.

? Quick quiz

1. Were children paid the same as adults?

2. How many hours did children work per day in textile mills in the USA?

3. When was it made illegal for children under the age of nine to work in UK factories?

See pages 132–133 for the answers

Child labour
Many children began work in factories as piecers, standing at the machines to repair breaks in the thread. Injuries were common.

Poor conditions
The machinery never stopped, so children often worked without breaks in cramped conditions, and with no protective clothing.

How much of the world did Europe colonize?

Between 1492 and 1914, European countries colonized over 80 percent of the world. Europe's overseas empires were often racist. Local people were treated badly, and their traditional ways of life were ignored. This led to rebellions and wars.

North America
Canada was a self-governing Dominion of the British Empire. Greenland and most Caribbean islands were ruled by their overseas colonizers.

Wheat was a major export from North America.

The empires of 1914
By 1914, few colonies remained in the Americas. Lands in Oceania, Asia, and Africa had been newly colonized in the 1800s–1900s. Use this key to learn who ruled where. in 1914.

- Britain
- France
- Portugal
- Spain
- Russia
- Italy
- Turkey
- Denmark
- Netherlands
- United States
- Belgium
- Germany

Goods such as bananas were grown in South America.

South America
The only remaining European colonies were British Guiana (now Guyana), Dutch Guiana (now Suriname), and French Guiana.

Why did countries build empires?

Raw materials, such as metals, from colonized lands could be sold by colonizers to make money. They could also gain control over trade routes, and access to soldiers and materials for war.

Quick quiz

1. Which countries had South American colonies in 1914?
2. Which empire was Finland part of in 1914?
3. Which country ruled India in 1914?

See pages 132–133 for the answers

Russia
The Russian Empire included Finland, much of Poland, and Siberia – from which sable fur (pictured) was an important export.

Southern Asia
From 1876 to 1948, the British monarch claimed to be the emperor of India. Indian cotton (pictured) was turned into cloth in British textile mills.

Africa
European powers rushed to rule Africa from the 1880s. Minerals, such as diamonds (pictured), could be mined in these lands.

Oceania
Australia and New Zealand were self-governing Dominions. Australia was a big exporter of wool and sheep.

102 EMPIRES AND REVOLUTIONS

What were they fighting about?

Government
President Abraham Lincoln (left, 1809–1865) wanted the whole nation to stay in the Union, which he led. The Confederates wanted to leave and form their own government, with their own laws.

Slavery
The Confederacy had 3.5 million enslaved workers, whose owners made money from the crops they grew. The Union wanted to end slavery. Their armies included formerly enslaved people.

Union States
In the Union, there were more people, railways, and factories making clothing and other items. This meant they had an advantage.

The US Civil War
The war lasted from 1861 to 1865, when the Union won. It was mainly fought in the South, and caused more US deaths than any other war.

Territories
Fighting spread to the western territories, which were not yet formal states of the USA.

Can a country go to war with itself?

When different groups within a country go to war over who should rule, it is called a civil war. The US Civil War was fought between Southern states, who formed the Confederacy, and Northern states, who formed the Union. They mainly argued over one thing – slavery.

Border States
The people living here were torn between both sides. The states still allowed slavery, but they stayed in the Union.

Gettysburg
The Confederates' advance northwards was halted here in July 1864, after a three-day battle. The Union did not lose a major battle after this.

1862 Antietam – most deaths

1861 Bull Run – first large battle

1862 Seven Pines – neither side wins

1863 Vicksburg – Union wins control of Mississippi river

1863 Port Hudson – 48-day siege

1861 Fort Sumter – first battle

Chancellorsville
This battle, in May 1864, was won by a Confederate army led by General Robert E. Lee (pictured). It showed his skill for planning fights, as he had the smaller army.

Confederate states
The Confederate states had 9 million people to draw soldiers from – less than half of the Union's 22 million people. But they had skilled generals.

Key
- Territories
- Confederate states
- Union states
- Key battle – Confederate win
- Key battle – Union win

Quick quiz
1. In which year did the US Civil War begin?
2. Who was president of the USA during the war?

See pages 132–133 for the answers

When were trains invented?

The Romans first built wagons that rolled along stone ruts (deep tracks) in the street. In the 1500s, miners in Europe built wooden tracks for horse-drawn wagons. Iron tracks followed, and then the steam train.

Steam power
English engineer Thomas Newcomen invented the first useful steam engine. It powered machinery that pumped water out of mines.

1712

1868

First mountain railway
The Mount Washington Cog in New Hampshire, USA, was the first mountain railway. The teeth of the train's cogwheel, or pinion, gripped a steep, slotted rail.

1879

First electric passenger train
The first electric passenger train was a demonstration model built by Werner von Siemens in Berlin, Germany. He went on to develop electric trams.

1890

First electric underground railway
The City and South London Railway in the UK was made electric in 1890. In 1900, France's Paris Métro opened, with electric-motor-powered carriages.

1912

First diesel locomotive
This locomotive was hard to start up and run. Diesel-electric engines followed, which used diesel to power a generator that made electricity.

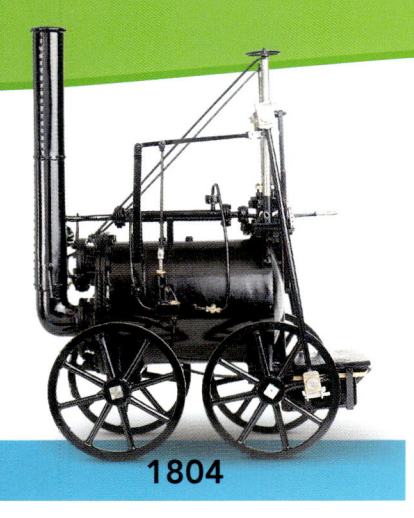

1804
First railway locomotive
Richard Trevithick's first steam locomotive carried 10 tonnes (11 tons) of iron and 50 men for 16 km (10 miles) in Wales.

1825
First public steam railway
England's Stockton and Darlington line was the first public railway. It hauled coal, and later passengers.

When were planes invented?
In 1903, Orville and Wilbur Wright flew the first heavier-than-air plane, the *Wright Flyer*, in North Carolina, USA. The flight lasted 12 seconds.

1863
First underground steam railway
The Metropolitan Line in London, UK, was the first of its kind. Vents carried engine fumes to the streets above, but it was still very smoky!

1830
First intercity railway
England's Liverpool and Manchester Railway was the first railway to run between two cities. It carried the locomotive *Rocket* – the best train of its day.

? True or false?
1. The first bullet train was invented in France.
2. The first underground train was powered by electricity.
3. The first heavier-than-air plane was invented by Wilbur and Orville Wright.

See pages 132–133 for the answers

1964
Bullet train
The design for this streamlined, high-speed Japanese train was copied for long-distance trains worldwide.

1994
The Channel Tunnel
This tunnel runs for almost 38 km (24 miles) under the sea between England and France. Japan's Seikan Tunnel is longer, but less of it is underwater.

2020
First driverless bullet train
This Chinese train can reach speeds of 350 kph (217 mph). It runs from Beijing to Zhangjiakou.

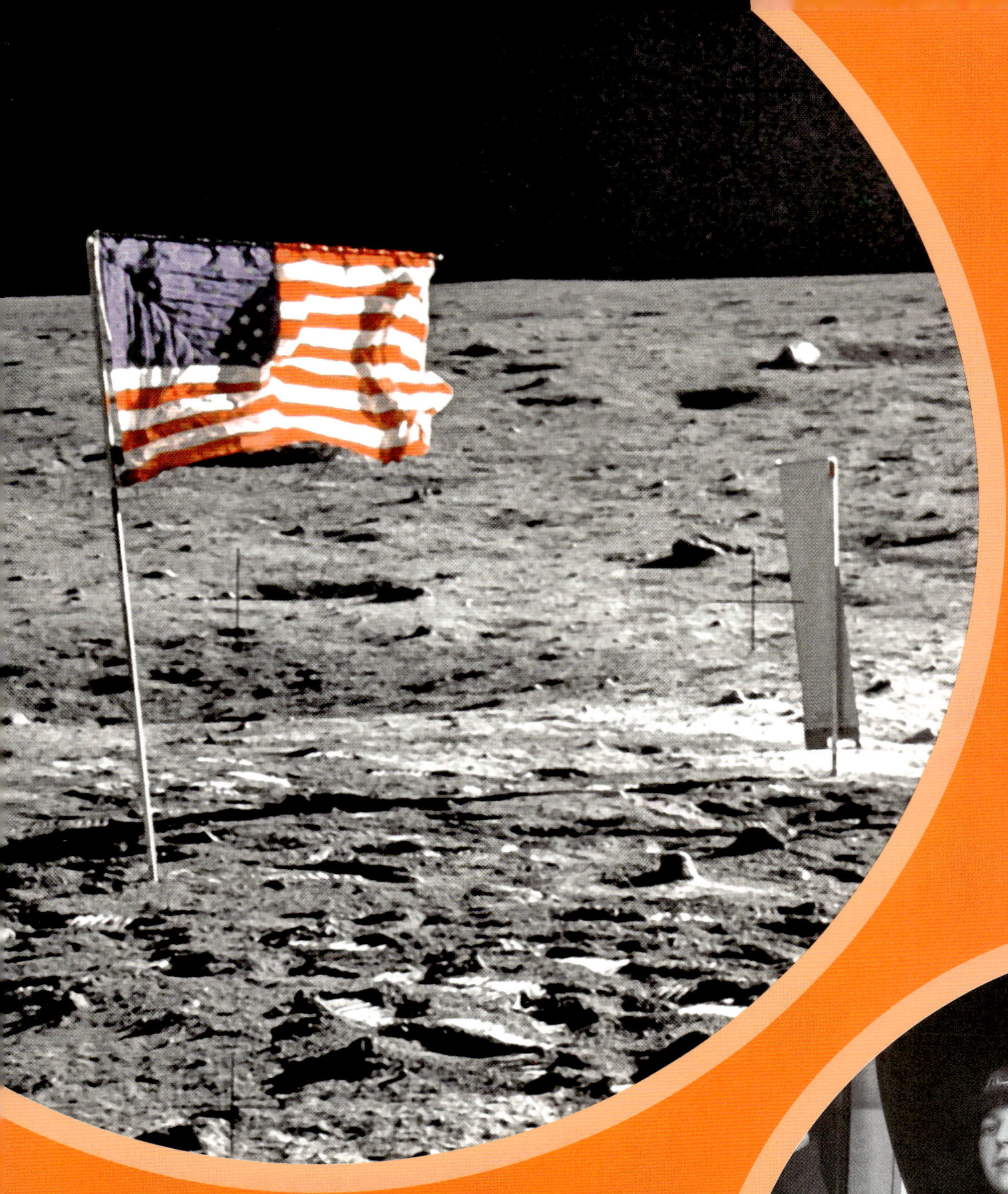

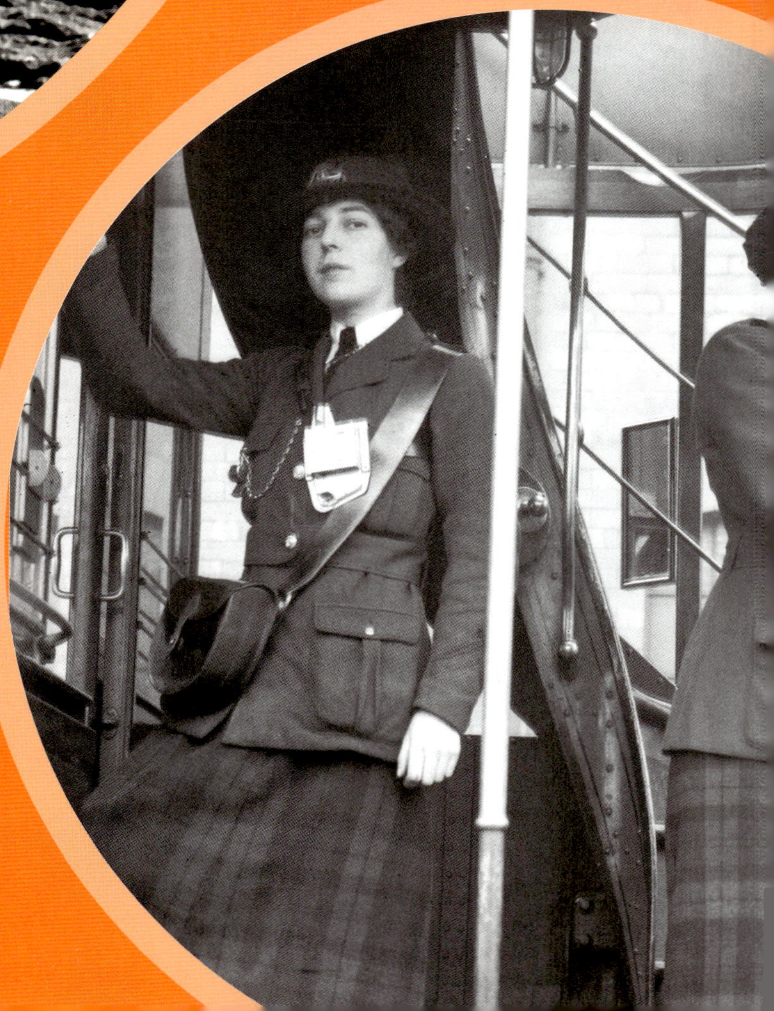

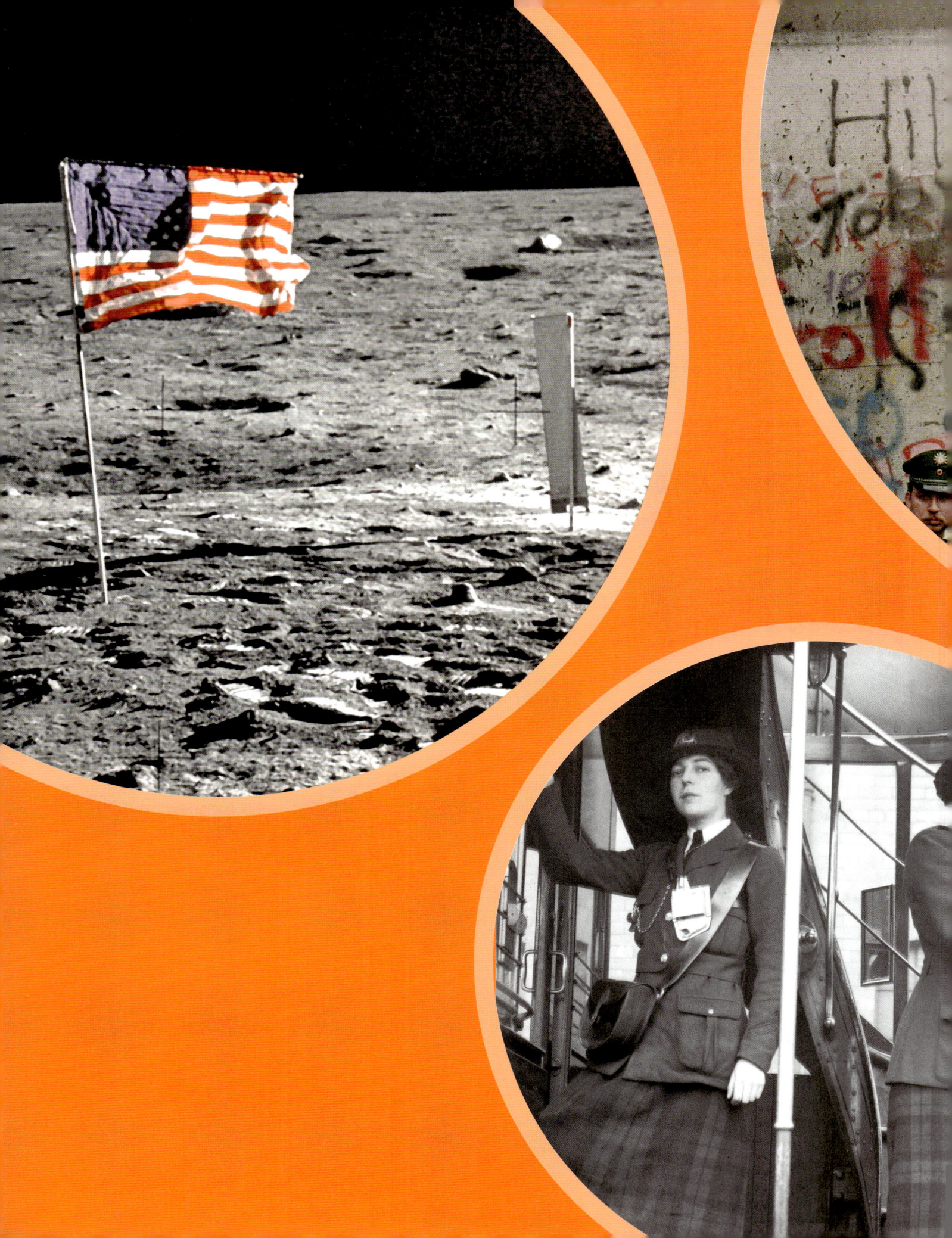

The modern world

Two expensive, ruinous world wars marked the early 20th century. But many countries won their freedom from European empires in the following years. The exploration of space began, and the world was transformed by electronic technology and scientific discoveries.

What was trench warfare?

World War One raged from 1914 to 1918, with most of the fighting taking place in Europe. In Western Europe, both sides dug long networks of trenches to protect themselves from gunfire. This was called the Western Front.

Leisure time
Letters from home kept up soldiers' spirits. They often spent downtime writing back, making up songs, or playing board games.

Conditions
Life in the muddy, rat-infested trenches was miserable. Many soldiers developed trench foot – a painful condition caused by always having wet feet.

Officers
Soldiers were led into battle and ordered to complete tasks in the trenches by officers.

Soldiers
They ate, slept, and worked in the trenches. Soldiers followed orders to mend walls or bail out floods, or to go over the top to battle.

Weapons
Before an attack on the ground, big guns would pound the enemy lines with shells. The troops were armed with rifles and bayonets.

No man's land
The land between the two sides was guarded with machine-guns pointing over the trench walls. There was nowhere to hide, here.

Quick quiz

1. Where was no-man's land?
2. What were German airships called?
3. Why did the Western Front go quiet on 11 November 1918?

See pages 132–133 for the answers

What technology was used in World War One?

Planes were used as fighters and bombers. The Germans also used huge airships, called zeppelins, to drop bombs. Britain was the first to use tanks, in 1916.

Who fought whom?
On one side were the Central Powers – the German, Ottoman, and Austria-Hungarian empire, and Bulgaria. On the opposite side were the Entente Powers – the French and British empires, Italy (from 1915), Romania, Russia, the USA (from 1917), and Japan.

- Allies
- Central powers
- Neutral countries

How did women get the vote?

Up until the late 19th century, women were not able to vote on who led their countries. But they fought to change this – writing books, and letters to politicians, and protesting until people took notice. Gradually, countries allowed women to vote.

Which country allowed women to vote first?

In New Zealand, Kate Sheppard called for women's suffrage (voting rights) over many years. She organized petitions and talked to politicians. Finally, in 1893, the country became the first to allow some women to vote in a national election.

Memorial for Kate Sheppard, New Zealand

Protests

Peaceful protests included marches, such as the one pictured here in the USA in 1913. Some women also used violence – such as bombing.

? Quick quiz

1. What does suffrage mean?
2. What is a ballot box?
3. Which country was the first to allow some women to vote in a national election?

See pages 132–133 for the answers

The first country to elect a female leader was Sri Lanka, in 1960.

Important thinkers

In 1792 an English writer called Mary Wollstonecraft (pictured) penned one of the first books about women's rights. This inspired other writers and campaigners.

Groups

Different groups sprang up to organize the fight. The British Suffragettes, led by Emmeline Pankhurst (above), used tactics such as arson – or setting fire to things.

World War One

In the UK during World War One, women took on jobs they would not normally have done. The public appreciated their work, and in 1918 some women were allowed the vote.

112 THE MODERN WORLD

The poor
Before 1917, most Russians worked on farms. If the weather changed and food could not grow, they would starve – while rich people ate well.

The tsars
Russians wanted to get rid of the tsar to bring about change. A revolution began in 1917, and this statue of a past tsar was beheaded.

Tsar Alexander III

Why did Russians revolt in 1917?

Life in early 20th-century Russia was hard. Most people earned little money, and often went hungry. Meanwhile, the tsar, or emperor, lived a life of luxury. When he did not listen to calls for change, people began to revolt.

Russian Revolution
The tsar of 1917, Nicholas II, had ignored peaceful protests throughout his reign. In 1905 his troops killed protestors, and anger grew.

Who was Karl Marx?

Karl Marx (1818–1883) was a German thinker who criticized how factory owners got rich selling goods made by underpaid workers. He thought that workers should have an equal share of money made, in a system called communism. Karl Marx inspired the Russian revolutionaries.

? Quick quiz

1. What was Russia renamed in 1922?
2. What colour is used for communist flags?

See pages 132–133 for the answers

Feb 1917
Queues for bread
The tsar sent farmers to fight in World War One, and food to feed them. Food shortages began, sparking big protests.

March 1917
First revolution
People stopped following the tsar's orders and there were mutinies by troops. He stepped down.

Nov 1917
Second revolution
Vladimir Lenin led a second revolution, against the new government. He overthrew them.

Dec 1922
Soviet Union
Vladimir Lenin renamed Russia the USSR (Union of Soviet Socialist Republics) – a communist country, led by Lenin.

Can money be worth nothing?

Money is anything that people agree can be used to pay for goods and services. Its value (the amount that it is worth) can go up or down. The way in which the money, industry, and trade of a country or region are organized makes up its economy.

Printing money
After World War One ended, Germany owed lots of money. The government printed more and more banknotes. Too much money going around meant that it was worth less.

What was the Great Depression?

Wall Street Crash
People can buy and sell parts of businesses, called shares, at a stock market. The crash of New York's stock market on Wall Street in 1929 helped lead to a depression (a severe downturn in the economy) called The Great Depression.

Dust-bowl USA
In the 1930s, a severe drought affected the US and Canadian prairies. Over-farming and soil erosion led to farmland being buried in dust. This caused great hardship and worsened the Great Depression.

Around the world
The Great Depression affected many parts of the world. These protestors marched all the way from Jarrow, in the northeast of England, to London, demanding work to feed their families.

❓ Quick quiz

1. What is an economic depression?

2. When did the Great Depression begin?

3. What was the name of the currency in Germany in 1918?

See pages 132–133 for the answers

Suffering citizens
Soon, a loaf of bread cost a whole suitcase of banknotes – and there were long queues at shops to get one.

Worthless cash
Because money was worth less, prices went up and up. This is called inflation. Farmers charged more for their produce, and workers demanded more for their labour.

Adolf Hitler (1889–1945)
Austrian-born Adolf Hitler led the racist German Nazi party to power in 1933. He started World War Two, and organized the mass murder of Jews, Roma, and other people he disliked.

Benito Mussolini (1883–1945)
In Italy, Benito Mussolini's Fascist Party used black-shirted militias to scare his opponents through violence. They marched on Rome in 1922.

Who were the dictators of 20th-century Europe?

A dictator is a ruler who is greedy for power and against freedom. After World War One, which cost lots of money and destroyed cities, there was great hardship and unrest in Europe. People were scared, which helped new, ruthless dictators to seize power.

Joseph Stalin (1878–1953)
Stalin took power in the USSR in 1922. He used secret police, imprisonments, and executions.

Francisco Franco (1892–1975)
Spain's General Franco started the Spanish Civil War (1936–1939) in order to gain power. He ruled from 1936–1975, terrorizing and executing many.

How do dictators stay in power?

By force
Violence, murder, and imprisonment can be used to scare and control people. In this photo, Joseph Stalin talks to the head of his secret police, who spied on people.

Fake news
Dictators control the news and, in modern times, social media. They use it to spread lies – making themselves seem good and blaming others for problems.

What is fascism?
This type of political movement supports dictatorship, extreme nationalism (celebration of its country), and war. Fascists oppose human rights and other types of government, and are often racist.

True or false?

1. Francisco Franco was a dictator of Italy.
2. Dictators use news and social media to tell lies.
3. Hitler and Mussolini both liked to be called "The Leader".

See pages 132–133 for the answers

How was World War Two fought?

The Second World War broke out between European countries, but quickly drew in other parts of the world. From 1939–1945, battles were fought with tanks and aircraft while submarines roamed the seas.

Where was World War Two fought?

War in Europe
A violent, racist group called the Nazis came to power in Germany in 1933, led by Adolf Hitler. The war broke out in Europe when Hitler invaded Poland, in 1939.

Nazi flags in Poland, 1939

War in the Pacific
In 1941, Japanese planes bombed Pearl Harbor, a US naval base. The USA joined the war, which now involved every continent.

The Pearl Harbor attack

In the sky
Planes fought in aerial battles. European cities were heavily bombed by enemy aircraft throughout the war.

German Messerschmitt Me 410 Hornisse

On land
Tank design had improved since World War One. The Battle of Kursk in 1943 involved 6,000 tanks.

German Panzer III medium tank

At sea
Battleships, armed with guns, bombarded one another in sea battles. Battleships were an important part of the Pacific war.

Japan's *Haruna* battleship

Underwater
Submarines were used to attack merchant and passenger ships as well as naval vessels. They fired torpedoes.

German U-boat

British Westland Lysander

USSR T-26 light tank

The USA's battleship *Missouri*

The USA's *Tang*

Who fought in World War Two?
The two sides were the Axis powers and the Allies. Countries joined the war at different times, and some stayed neutral (did not join a side).

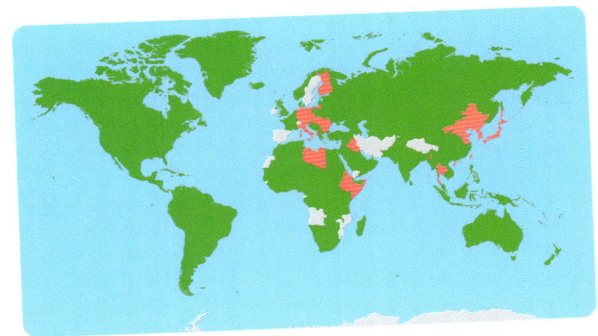

🟩 Allies – France, Britain, the USSR, the USA, China, and 10 other nations

🟥 Axis – Germany, Italy, Japan, and seven other nations

⬜ Neutral

? Quick quiz

1. Where is Pearl Harbor?
   a) In the Atlantic Ocean
   b) In the North Sea
   c) In the Pacific Ocean

2. When did World War Two begin?
   a) 1918
   b) 1939
   c) 1945

See pages 132–133 for the answers

How did India get rid of British rule?

Many colonized countries won their freedom in the 1900s, some through wars, and some peacefully. After centuries of protest against British rule, India became independent as the nations of India and Pakistan in 1947.

When did South Africa decolonize?

South Africa won independence from Britain in 1910, but the vote was not given to non-white citizens. From 1948–1991, there was a policy of apartheid (racial separation). Nelson Mandela (pictured) became the country's first Black president in 1994.

Indian National Congress

The Indian National Congress was founded in 1885 to campaign for Indian civil rights. In the 1900s it became more radical and called more for independence.

Activists

Many individual people took action to win freedom for their country. One such was Sarojini Naidu (pictured with Gandhi), who spoke against British rule in front of large crowds.

Since 1945, 80 former colonies have won their freedom.

? Quick quiz

1. When did India and Pakistan become independent?
2. What was the name for racial segregation in South Africa?

See pages 132–133 for the answers

Mahatma Gandhi

Mohandas K. Gandhi (1869–1948), known as Mahatma, meaning "great-souled", became a popular figure who called for self-rule and led peaceful protests.

Historical struggles

The fight for Indian independence began in the 1700s, when the British started taking control of the Indian subcontinent. Tipu Sultan led the Anglo-Mysore Wars against the British from 1767–1799.

THE MODERN WORLD

Can sitting down change the world?

In 1955, Rosa Parks was getting a bus home from work in Montgomery, USA. The driver ordered the African-American woman to give up her seat to a white man. She refused – inspiring others to fight back against racism in the USA.

Segregation
In the 1950s, Black and white people in the USA were often kept separate. This was called segregation.

Who was Martin Luther King Jr?

Martin Luther King Jr (1929–1968) was a leader in the US civil rights movement. He called for an end to segregation, and equal rights in education, voting, and work.

Civil rights
Even after slavery ended, African Americans continued to be treated badly in the USA. The civil rights movement fought against this treatment.

1960
Greensboro sit-in
After being refused service at a lunch counter, Black students refused to leave. Other protestors used this tactic.

The Rosa Parks effect

After 11 months, the top court in the USA ruled that the bus company had broken the law. Rosa had won the right for anyone to sit where they liked. She showed that protesting worked.

? Quick quiz

1. What is a sit-in?
2. When was the Civil Rights Act signed?
3. What were the Jim Crow laws?

See pages 132–133 for the answers

The Montgomery Bus Boycott, sparked by Rosa's actions, was the first major civil rights protest.

1960

New Orleans school
Ruby Bridges, aged just six, became the first African American to register for an all-white school.

1963

Great March on Washington, D.C.
Martin Luther King Jr called for equality to a crowd of 250,000 people, marching in the capital.

1964

Civil Rights Act
This law protects civil rights, such as the right to vote, for all – regardless of race, religion, or gender.

THE MODERN WORLD

What was the Cold War?

Between 1947 and 1991, a war took place in which the two sides did not fight battles against one another. On one side were the USA and Western Europe. On the other side were countries in the Soviet Union, Eastern Europe, and China.

? Quick quiz

1. When did the Berlin Wall come down?
2. What is an arms race?
3. What did moles do in the Cold War?

See pages 132–133 for the answers

The USSR
The USSR and its allies were communist states. This meant that people worked for the state, and were housed and looked after in return.

Nikita Khrushchev (leader of the USSR from 1953 to 1964)

Spies
Spies were used to find out about the other side's secrets. They used codes and hidden cameras, and stole the designs of new weapons.

The nuclear arms race
Each side built more and more nuclear weapons, to scare their opponents. But if one side fired, so would the other – so neither did.

The Cuban Missile Crisis
In 1962, the two sides placed nuclear missiles in places near their opponents – with the USSR using Cuba. In the end, they both agreed to remove them.

When did the USSR break up?

By the late 1980s, many people in the USSR were protesting against its leaders. In 1989, the Berlin Wall, which stopped people escaping from the USSR-run East Germany, fell. The USSR broke up in 1991.

John F. Kennedy (US president from 1961 to 1963)

The USA
Along with its allies, the USA wanted to stop the spread of communism. They believed in capitalism – a type of society in which private companies seek to make money for themselves.

North Korea flag

South Korea flag

South Vietnam flag

The Berlin Wall
In 1949, Germany was split into two nations. In 1961, USSR-run East Germany built a wall in the capital to stop its people escaping to West Berlin, which was run by its rivals.

The Korean War
From 1950, North Korea, supported by the USSR and China, fought South Korea, backed by the USA and the UN. The war ended in 1953.

The Vietnam War
From 1954–73, South Vietnam and the USA fought to stop North Vietnam from uniting the country as a communist state – which happened in 1976.

North Vietnam flag

What was the Space Race?

The first two countries to explore space were the USSR (now Russia) and the USA. They were fierce rivals, and from 1955 to 1975 each tried to get ahead of the other in what became known as the Space Race.

What was Saturn V?
In 1969, this mighty, three-stage rocket lifted three US astronauts into space, as part of the *Apollo 11* mission. The modules travelled on towards lunar orbit.

First man in space
The first man in space was a Russian called Yuri Gagarin, in 1962. He completed a single orbit of Earth in his spacecraft, *Vostok 1*.

First craft in space
The Space Race was set off in 1957, when the Russians successfully launched a simple satellite (an unpiloted craft) called *Sputnik 1*. It orbited (circled) the Earth.

First dog in space
A stray terrier called Laika was the first animal astronaut, on *Sputnik 2* in 1958. Sadly, she did not survive the journey.

Saturn V

Lunar modules

First woman in space
In 1963, Russian Valentina Tereshkova became the first woman in space. She orbited the Earth 48 times in just under three days.

Moon landing
On this US mission, Neil Armstrong (pictured) and Buzz Aldrin landed in the lunar module. Neil walked on the Moon first, and they both collected rock samples.

How do we know what's in outer space?

Voyager 1
This US probe was launched in 1977. It flew by Jupiter, by Saturn and its moon Titan, and left our Solar System in 2012. It is still sending back information today.

Hubble Space Telescope
A US-European project, this space telescope was launched in 1990. It showed points in the Universe further away than we had ever seen.

? Quick quiz

1. What was the name of the *Apollo 11* Lunar Module?

2. Who was the first woman in space?

See pages 134–135 for the answers

128 THE MODERN WORLD

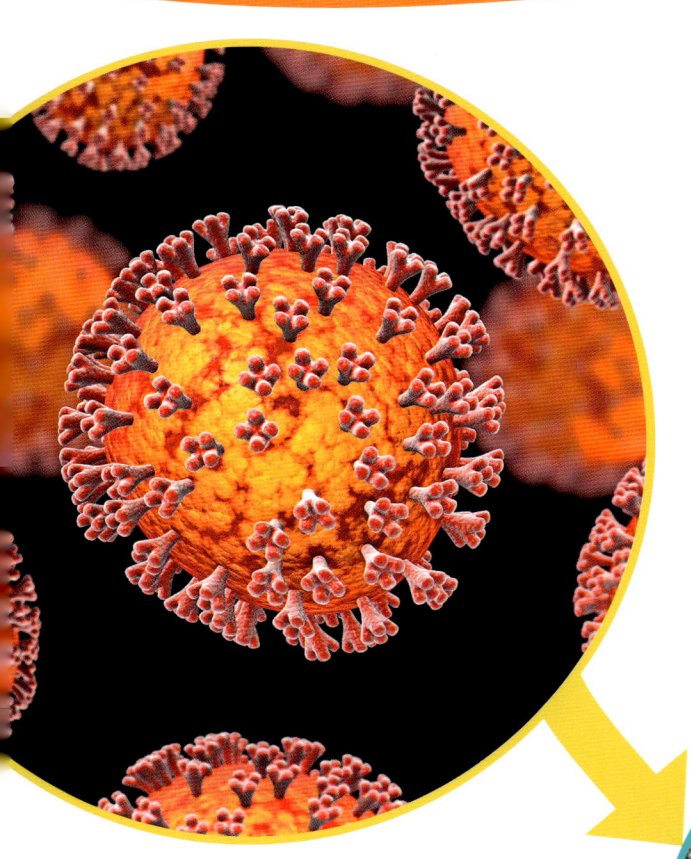

What have been the worst pandemics in history?

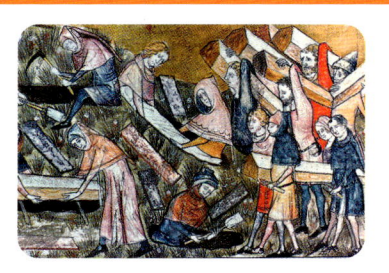

The Black Death, or plague, killed 75–200 million people across Asia and Europe between 1346-1353. It returned many times in later centuries, in various forms.

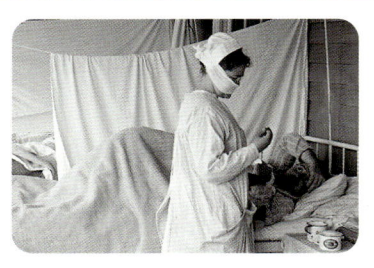

The Great Influenza of 1918–1920 killed at least 50 million in a world already ravaged by war. It is sometimes called the "Spanish flu".

The birth of COVID-19

There are lots of different types of coronavirus disease – but the one that began spreading in December 2019 was called COVID-19. It is related to viruses that affect bats, and affects the lungs and other parts of the body.

Spreading worldwide

COVID-19 was first reported in China, but quickly spread worldwide through air travel. The first wave of COVID-19 was the deadliest, especially amongst older people.

What is a pandemic?

Infectious diseases have changed history. If they kill many people, they can bring an end to states and trade, as well as everyday life. Diseases that spread to many countries are called pandemics – for example, the COVID-19 virus that began to spread in 2019.

Pandemics through time

Pandemics have caused huge devastation throughout history. But we have developed better medicines to deal with them over time.

? Quick quiz

1. When did the COVID-19 pandemic begin?
2. How many people were killed by the Great Influenza?
3. Has any pandemic virus been completely defeated?

See pages 132–133 for the answers

Stopping the spread

COVID-19 is spread by particles in the air. Protective equipment such as face masks, testing, and isolation are all ways of stopping the spread.

Vaccine developed

A vaccine stops someone getting a virus. The first COVID-19 vaccines were developed very quickly, in 2020, but they needed to be boosted and adapted, as new strains (versions) of the virus developed.

1400s
Black Death
This disease was spread by rat fleas. Beaked masks were thought to protect against it.

1870–1874
Smallpox
There had been many smaller outbreaks of this rash-causing disease before it became a pandemic in Europe.

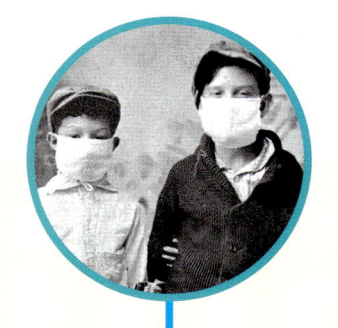

1918–1920
Influenza
This disease is common today, and not usually deadly. But when it first appeared, in 1918, it killed millions.

2019–
COVID-19
This disease quickly spread worldwide, but a vaccine was soon developed to fight it.

130 THE MODERN WORLD

How can we make history?

The world can change very much in a single lifetime. History is ongoing, and we are all part of it. Inventions, scientific discoveries, and new pieces of art can all add to it – whether they are a stranger's or your own!

? Quick quiz

1. When was the ENIAC made?
   a) 1945
   b) 1958
   c) 1993

2. When was the World Wide Web invented?
   a) 1989
   b) 1991
   c) 1995

See pages 132–133 for the answers

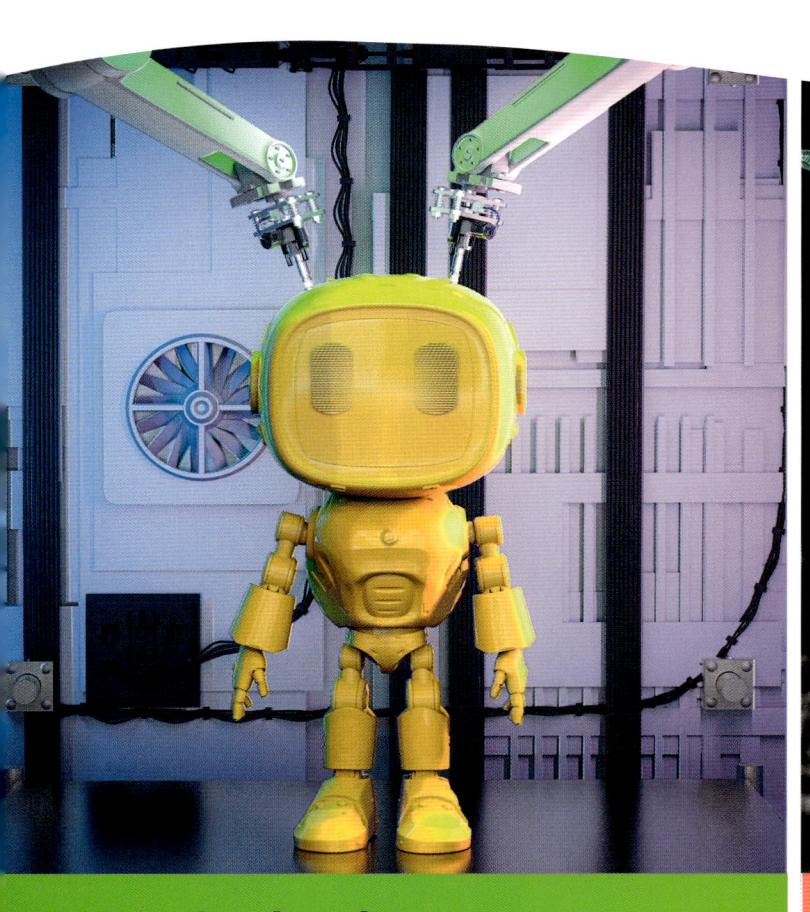

New technology
You have read in this book about how technology, from metalworking to factory machines, can change history. Since the 1980s, we've improved computers and printed 3D objects, and there is much more tech to come.

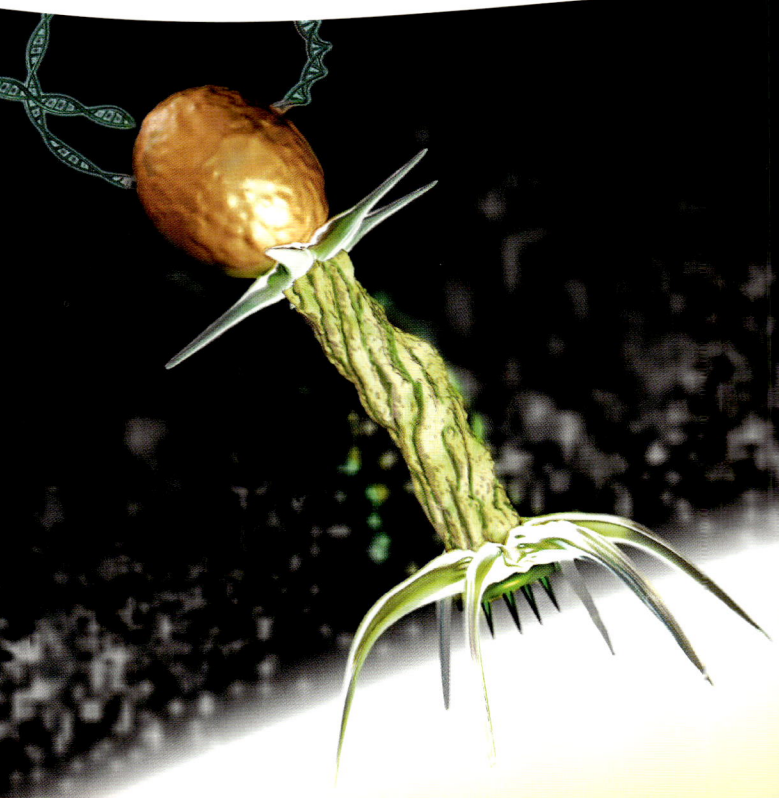

Scientific discoveries
Since the 1950s, we have gone from discovering the structure of deoxyribonucleic acid (DNA) – the chemical that passes on features such as hair colour from parent to child – to finding DNA-based treatments for cancer (above). What's next?

Which modern inventions changed everything?

Computers
The first programmable digital computer was the giant ENIAC, in 1945. New inventions, such as microchips (1958), made computers smaller and smaller. Smartphones were invented in 1993.

The World Wide Web
The World Wide Web (the pages on the internet) was developed in 1989, to share information between universities. It has since transformed the way we learn, communicate, and entertain ourselves.

Artificial intelligence (AI)
Research into intelligent machines began in the 1950s. Machines can now do many things that once only humans could do – understand speech, drive cars, play chess, and more.

Governments and laws
Historical changes can be brought in by governments – for example, racist actions can be banned. In many countries, adults can choose who represents them in the government, using secret votes cast in ballot boxes.

Calling for change
It is up to all of us to bring about change in our communities, for example by protesting. We must make sure our leaders are doing what is right. We must challenge the powerful, and protect the freedoms that movements in the past have won.

Answers

Page 7 1) An archaeologist studies things from the past. 2) An object made by humans. 3) No.

Page 11 1) False. Dinosaurs were extinct by 65 million years ago. 2) False. The first humans lived in Africa. 3) True.

Page 13 1) True. 2) False. It was built from about 3100 BCE. 3) True.

Page 15 1) A stepped temple. 2) Cuneiform. 3) The Tigris and the Euphrates.

Page 17 1) True. 2) False. Anubis was the god of mummification.

Page 18 1) The Nile. 2) A type of pottery. 3) In what is now Nigeria, West Africa.

Page 21 1) True. 2) False. Bronze is a mixture of copper and tin.

Page 23 The silk moth.

Page 25 1) Cadiz. 2) Sea-snail slime. 3) Lebanon. It was once part of Phoenicia.

Page 27 1) Grown-up males. 2) No, it was made up of many independent states. 3) It means "rule of the people".

Page 29 1) Persia. 2) Darius I. 3) Alexandria.

Page 31 1) Underground. Special lifts were built to carry them up to the arena. 2) Gladiators. 3) 50,000.

Page 32 1) A dome-like, Buddhist monument. 2) Ashoka's lion capital. 3) Hinduism.

Page 35 1) Yes, they number about 6 million. 2) Egyptian. 3) A cenote.

Page 37 1) The Pacific. 2) East Asia. 3) The USA.

Page 41 1) The belief in more than one god. 2) About 4,000 years old. 3) Christianity.

Page 42 1) The Greeks. 2) Constantine. 3) Turkey.

Page 45 1) about 6,500 km (4,000 miles). 2) Around four years. 3) Chang'an (now Xi'an), ancient China.

Page 47 1) France. 2) Ostrogoths.

Page 49 1) William I. 2) Thor. 3) Dragon heads.

Page 51 1) Cyrillic. 2) Poland.

Page 53 1) 14. 2) A sport in which horse riders try to dismount each other with lances. 3) It was called chivalry.

Page 54 1) An area ruled by a caliph. 2) 120,000 km (75,000 miles). 3) The Umayyad caliphate.

Page 57 1) A type of tent. 2) Large, flat grasslands without trees. 3) Khubilai Khan.

Page 59 1) The Shang Dynasty. 2) The Yuan Dynasty.

Page 61 1) The *daimyo*. 2) Steel. 3) No, female warriors in feudal Japan were called onna-musha, not samurai!

Page 63 1) "Korea" comes from the name of the Goryeo, or Koryo dynasty. 2) The Joseon Dynasty. 3) North Korea and South Korea.

Page 65 1) Cambodia. 2) Buddhism and Hinduism. 3) Foreign merchants.

Page 67 1) Timbuktu. 2) Ruler. 3) Nigeria.

Page 69 A bird.

Page 70 1) Yes. 2) They rode horses brought over by Europeans. 3) The northwest coast of North America.

Page 73 1) Mexico. 2) Eagles and jaguars. 3) Yes.

Page 75 1) False, Cusco was the capital. 2) False, they used llamas. 3) True.

Page 79 1) It means rebirth. 2) 4 million. 3) In the Louvre Museum in Paris, France.

Page 80 1) The Vikings. 2) The king and queen of Spain. 3) About three years.

Page 83 1) 1620. 2) New Amsterdam.

Page 85 1) A Muslim ruler. 2) 334 years. 3) No, despite his attempts!

Page 87 1) True. 2) True. 3) False, they are buried there.

Page 89 1) Around 60,000 years ago. 2) Hunting. 3) 1788.

Page 93 1) In 1773. 2) It was when the USA declared independence in 1776. 3) The Treaty of Paris, 1783.

Page 95 1) It commemorates the storming of the Bastille in 1789. 2) Marie Antoinette. 3) Blue, white, and red.

Page 97 1) 1849. 2) 1866. 3) Because slavery was illegal in Canada during the railroad years.

Page 99 1) No, they were paid less. 2) 10–14 hours. 3) 1833.

Page 101 1) England, France, and The Netherlands. 2) The Russian Empire. 3) Britain.

Page 103 1) 1861. 2) Abraham Lincoln.

Page 105 1) False. It was invented in Japan. 2) False. It was powered by steam. 3) True.

Page 109 1) No-man's land was between the trenches occupied by each side. 2) Zeppelins. 3) Because the war had ended.

Page 110 1) The right to vote. 2) A box for placing votes. 3) New Zealand.

Page 113 1) The USSR. 2) Red.

Page 115 1) A severe downturn in an economy. 2) 1929. 3) The Mark.

Page 117 1) False, Francisco Franco was a dictator of Spain. 2) True. 3) True.

Page 119 1) In the Pacific Ocean. 2) 1939.

Page 120 1) 1947. 2) Apartheid.

Page 123 1) When people refuse to move from a place as a protest. 2) 2 July, 1964. 3) A set of laws enforcing segregation in the USA.

Page 124 1) 1989. 2) A race to build weapons. 3) Moles were people that worked for the enemy from inside a country, passing back information.

Page 127 1) *Eagle*. 2) Valentina Tereshkova.

Page 129 1) 2019. 2) More than 50 million. 3) Yes. Smallpox was eradicated because of a vaccine.

Page 130 1) 1945. 2) 1989.

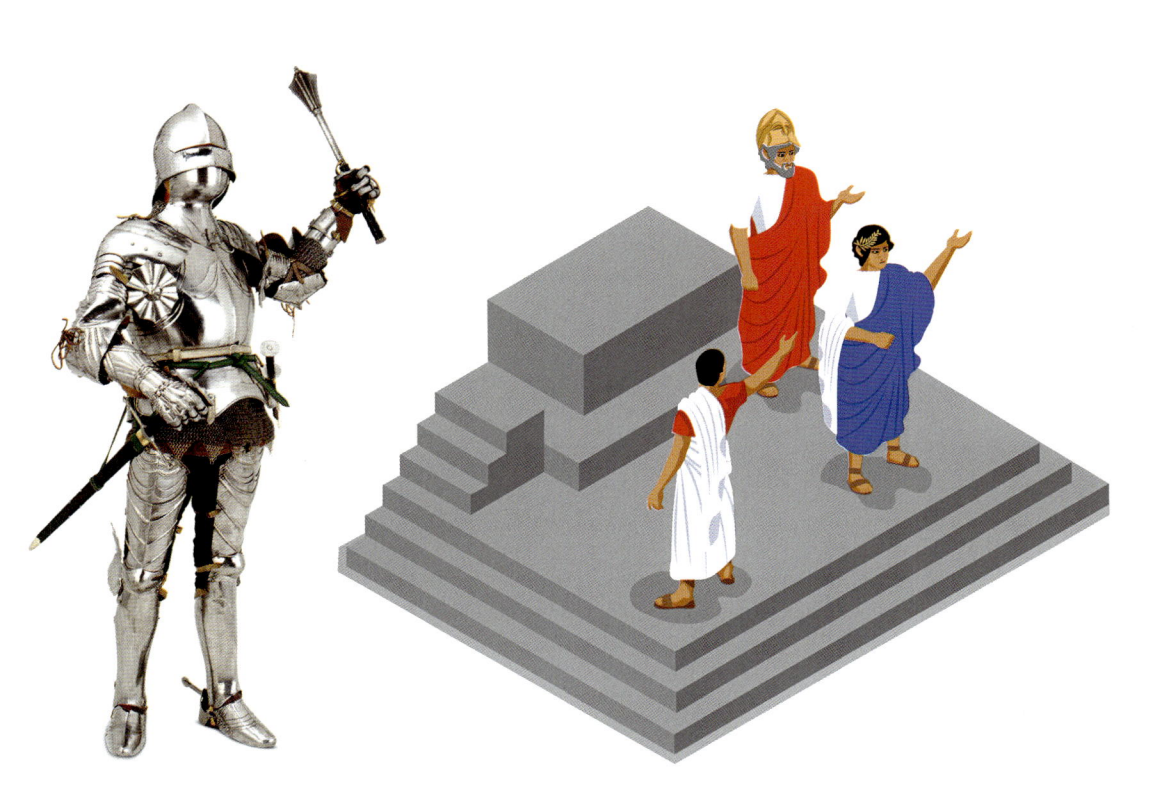

Quiz your friends!

Who knows the most about history? Test your friends and family with these tricky questions. See pages 136–137 for the answers.

Questions

1. What was a Viking chieftain called?

8. Which **religion began** in India with the teachings of **Guru Nanak**?

2. Who were the conductors of the Underground Railroad?

3. WHAT IS JOUSTING?

4. Who painted the Mona Lisa?

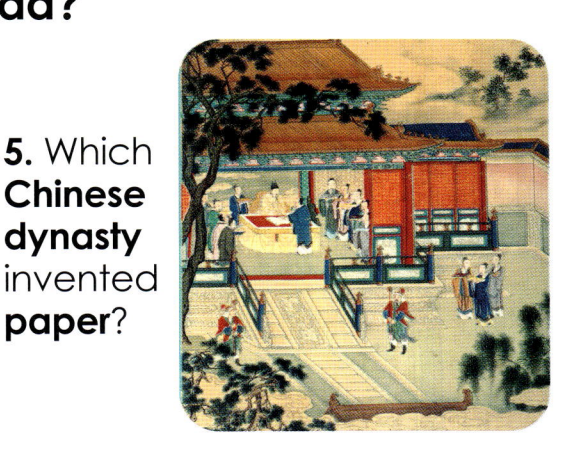

5. Which Chinese dynasty invented paper?

6. What was the Samurai long sword called?

7. What was the name of the first animal astronaut?

9. In which year did the Wright brothers fly the first heavier-than-air plane?

10. WHO WERE THE GLADIATORS?

11. What did Tim Berners-Lee invent that changed the way we learn, communicate, and entertain ourselves?

12. IN WHICH YEAR WAS THE COVID-19 VACCINE INVENTED?

13. Whose actions sparked the Montgomery Bus Boycott?

14. Which Hindu temple is the largest religious site in the world?

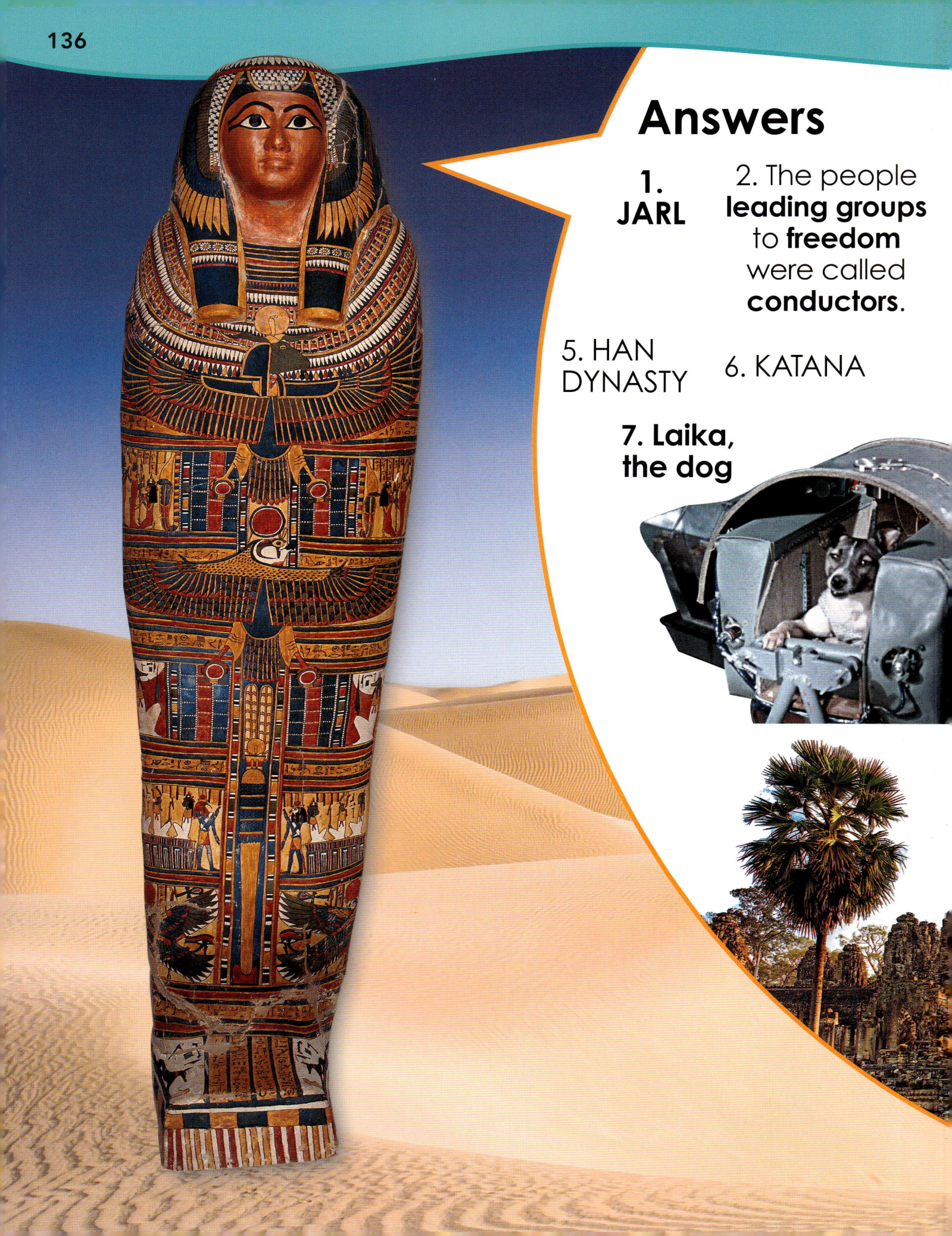

Answers

1. JARL

2. The people leading groups to **freedom** were called **conductors**.

5. HAN DYNASTY

6. KATANA

7. Laika, the dog

137

3. A sport where riders try to dismount each other with lances.

4. LEONARDO DA VINCI

8. SIKHISM

9. 1903

10. Well-trained fighters who fought each other or **wild animals**.

11. The World Wide Web

12. 2020

13. ROSA PARKS

14. ANGKOR WAT

Glossary

Allies
People or countries working together. In World War I and II, the Allies were the countries fighting Germany and other forces

Ancestor
Person who lived in the past, and who is a distant relative of people who are alive today

Architecture
Art of designing buildings or structures

Arena
Enclosed area with seats used for sports or other forms of entertainment

Bible
The holy book of the Christian religion

Buddhism
Religion and philosophy based on the teachings of the Buddha

C.
Short for circa, the Latin word for "about"

Capital
Main town or city of a country or area, usually where the government is based

Capitalism
System in which businesses are owned by individuals and not by the country or government

Cast
To make an object by pouring hot, liquid metal into a mould

Christian
Someone who follows the religion of Christianity, which is based on the teachings of Jesus Christ

Citizen
Person who belongs to a city or a bigger community, such as a state or country

City state
City and its surrounding territory that has its own government

Civil rights
Group of rights for people in a community, such as the right to be treated the same way as others

Civilization
Group of people living together in a complex society

Colonize
To take control of another country or region, and send settlers to live there

Communism
Political system in which everything belongs to the state, or government. The wealth and products of the state are divided between its citizens

Conquer
To take control of a place by force

Decolonize
Process of becoming a free country, having once been ruled by another country

Descendant
Someone who is related to a person or group of people who lived in the past

Dictator
Ruler of a country who has total power

Elect
To choose by voting

Empire
Several regions or countries controlled by one person or country

Export
Something that has been sent abroad to be traded or sold

Feudal system
Social structure during the Middle Ages in which people worked and fought for a ruler and in return were given a safe place to live

Fine
To charge someone an amount of money as punishment for not obeying a rule or law

Government
Group of people who run a country, for example, by making its laws

Henge
Circular or oval enclosure created during the Neolithic and Bronze Ages, often containing stones or wooden pillars

Islamic
Belonging or relating to the religion of Islam

Isolation
State of being alone

Ivory
Hard, white tusk of an animal, such as an elephant

Locomotive
Vehicle at the front or back of a train that pulls or pushes the carriages along

Mammoth
One of the largest land animals that lived during the Stone Age

Medieval
Relating or belonging to the Middle Ages, a time in European history between the years c.500–1500 CE

Merchant
Someone who trades (swaps) or sells goods

Mesopotamia
Greek term meaning "between rivers", which is used to describe the ancient land between the Tigris and Euphrates rivers

Monument
Building, statue, or structure with historical importance

Mosque
Place of prayer for people who follow the religion of Islam

Offering
Something that has been offered in worship or devotion to a god

Pilgrimage
Journey to a sacred place for religious reasons

Predator
Animal that hunts and eats other animals

Prophet
Religious teacher, believed to be a messenger of God

Protest
Act that shows disagreement with something

Pyramid
Stone structure with a square base and sloping sides, which can either be straight or stepped. Pyramids were often built as temples and tombs

Relatives
Members of a family group

Religion
System of belief in a god or gods. Most religions involve rituals and ceremonies of some kind

Republic
Type of country or state, with a leader or leaders chosen by the people

Revolution
Sudden overthrow of a government or way of life

Sacred
Considered holy, possibly related to a god or goddess

Sacrifice
Act of giving up something, or killing an animal or person for a religious ceremony

Sahara
The largest desert in the world, which covers a huge area of North Africa

Scholar
Person who is considered an expert in a subject

Settlement
Place where people have settled down and built homes

Site
Area of land on which something is located

State
Country, or region within a country, that has its own government

Tax
Money paid to the government to help it run the country

Trade
The swapping, or buying and selling, of items

Treaty
Agreement between two or more countries

Vote
To formally choose someone or something

Worship
To honour and show respect to a god or holy object

Index

3D printing 130

A
aircraft 78, 105, 109, 118–19
Aldrin, Buzz 127
Alexander the Great 29
Alexandria 29
American Revolutionary War 92–3
Angkor Wat 64
Angles 47
apartheid 120
Apollo 11 126–7
archaeology 6
architecture 74, 86–7, 78, 79
Armstrong, Neil 126
art 7, 85, 79
artificial intelligence 131
Ashoka, Emperor 33
Athens 26, 27
Australia 88–9, 101
Austro-Hungarian Empire 109
Axis powers 119
Axum 19
Ayutthaya Kingdom 64, 65
Aztecs 72–3

B
Babylon 14
Baekje Kingdom 63
Baghdad 55, 85
barbarians 46–7
Bastille, storming of the 94
Belarus 51
Benin, Kingdom of 66, 67
Berlin Wall 125
Black Death 128, 129
Borobudur 64
Boston Tea Party 92
Bridges, Ruby 123
Britain 47, 82–3, 92–3, 100–1, 109, 120
Bronze Age 20–1
Buddhism 33, 40, 45, 58, 64–5
Bulgaria 51, 109
bullet trains 105
Byzantine Empire 42–3, 44

C
caliphates 54–5
Canada 97, 100
canopic jars 17
Carthage 25
castles 53
cave paintings 12, 89
Celts 21, 47
Central Powers 109
Chandragupta Maurya 32, 33
Chang'an 45, 58
Channel Tunnel 105
Charlemagne, Emperor 46
Chichen Itza 34
Christianity 40, 41
Circus Maximus 31
civil rights 121, 122–3
Civil Rights Act (USA, 1964) 123
Civil War, US 102–3
Cold War 124–5
colonies 91, 82–3, 92–3, 100–1, 120–1, 82–3, 92–3
Colosseum 30–1
Columbus, Christopher 80
communism 113, 124–5

computers 131
Confederate States 102–3
Confucianism 62
Constantine, Emperor 42
Constantinople 39, 42–3, 44
coronavirus 128–9
Cortés, Hernán 73
cotton mills 98–9
Covid-19 128–9
Cree people 71
Croatia 51
Crusades 43
Cuban missile crisis 124
Czech Republic 51

D
da Gama, Vasco 81
Declaration of Independence 93
decolonization 120–1
democracy 26–7
dictators 116–17
disease 77, 128–9
DNA 130
Dreaming, the 89

E

East Germany 125
economy 114–15
education 98, 122, 123
Egyptians, ancient 16–17, 18, 19, 41
El Castillo 34–5

F

factories 98–9, 113, 130
fake news 117
farming 12, 13, 14, 48, 72, 75, 89, 112, 114, 115
fascism 116, 117
First Australians 88–9
food
    Aztec 73
    First Australians 89
    prices 114–15
    Stone Age 12, 13
Franco, General Francisco 117
France 47, 54, 82, 92, 94–5, 100, 109
Franks 46
French Revolution 94–5
Frisians 47

G

Gaelic 47
Gagarin, Yuri 126
games 15
Gandhi, Mohandas K 120–1
Genghis Khan 57
gladiators 30–1
gods 41
    Aztec 72
    Viking 48–9
Goguryeo Kingdom 63
gold 66, 67
government 131
    ancient Greece 26–7
    votes for women 110–11
Great Depression 114–15
Great Wall of China 22, 59
Great Zimbabwe 68–9
Greece, ancient 26–7, 28, 29, 42, 78, 79
Greensboro sit-in 122
guillotine 95

H

Hagia Sophia 43
Haida people 70
Han Dynasty 59
Harappa 15
Harun al-Rashid, Caliph 55
Hausa kingdoms 66
Hellenistic World 29
Hinduism 41, 64, 65
Hitler, Adolf 116, 118
Hubble Space Telescope 127
Hungary 84
hunting 13, 71, 98

I

Ibn Battuta 54
Incas 74–5
India 32–3, 86–7, 101, 120–1
independence movements 120–1
Indus Valley 15
industrialization 98, 130
inflation 115
influenza 128, 129
Inuit 71
inventions
    Chinese 23, 45, 58, 59
    Korean 62–3
    Leonardo da Vinci 78
    modern 130–1
Ireland 47
Iron Age 20–1
Islam 40, 41, 54–5
Istanbul 43
Italy 47, 78–9, 116
ivory 18, 19, 24, 85
ivory 18, 19, 24, 85

J

Java 64, 65
Jews, persecution of 116
Joseon Dynasty 62–3
Judaism 40, 116
Jutes 47

K

Kennedy, John F 125
Khmer Empire 64
Khrushchev, Nikita 124
kimchi 63
King, Martin Luther Jr 122, 123
knights 52–3
Korea 62–3
Korean War 125
Khubilai Khan 57, 59
Kush 18–19

L
lacrosse 70
Laika 126
law 131
Lenin, Vladimir 113
Leonardo da Vinci 78–9
Liao Dynasty 58
Lincoln, Abraham 102
Lombards 47
Louis XVI of France 95

M
Machu Picchu 74–5
Magellan, Ferdinand 81
Majapahit Empire 65
Mali Empire 66–7
Mandela, Nelson 120
Mansa Musa 66–7
Māori 37
March on Washington 123
Marie Antoinette, Queen of France 95
Marx, Karl 113
Mataram Kingdom 64
Mauryan Empire 32–3
Maya 34–5
megaliths 12
Meroë 19
Mesopotamia 14, 20
metalwork 20–1, 130
Middle East 48, 54, 85
mines 98
Ming Dynasty 59
Mohenjo-Daro 15
money 22, 114–15
Mongol Empire 56–7, 59, 63
monotheism 41
Montgomery Bus Boycott 122–3
Moon landings 127
Mughal Empire 86–7
Muhammad, the Prophet 41, 54, 55
mummification 16–17
Mussolini, Benito 116

N
Napoleon I, Emperor 95
navigation 37, 80
Nazi party 116, 118
Netherlands 82, 100
New Zealand 101, 110
Nicholas II of Russia 112
nobles 52
Nok 18
Normans 49
nuclear arms race 124

O
Oceania 101
Olmecs 35
Oregon Trail 83
Ostrogoths 46, 47
Ottoman Empire 43, 84–5, 109

P
Pakistan 120
Pankhurst, Emmeline 111
Parks, Rosa 122–3
Pearl Harbor 118
Persian Empire 28–9
Phoenicians 24–5
piracy 81
plague 45, 128, 129
Poland 51, 101, 118
Polo, Marco 44
Polynesians 36–7
polytheism 41
Portugal 54, 81
Powhattan people 71
propaganda 117
protests 120, 121, 131
Pueblo peoples 70
Punt 18
Puritans 82
pyramids, American 34–5, 73

Q
Qin Dynasty 59
Qin Shi Huang 22–3
Qing Dynasty 59
quipus 75

R
racism 100, 117, 120, 122–3, 131
religions 40–1
Renaissance 78–9
Rhodes 84
roads 23, 28
Roma 116
Romania 109
Romans 25, 30–1, 42, 46, 47, 78, 79, 104
Rome, fall of 39, 43, 46
roundhouses 20–1
runes 47
Russian Revolution 112–13

S
sacrifices 72, 73
Samurai 60–1
Saturn V 126–7
Saxons 47
science 78, 107, 130
Scotland 47
secret police 117
segregation 122
Serbia 51
Shah Jahan, Emperor 86
Shang Dynasty 59
shelters 13
ships 24–5, 36–7, 118–19
shoguns 60
Shona people 68
Siberia 101
Sikhism 40
Silk Road 39, 44–5
Silla Kingdom 63
slavery 48, 67, 77, 82, 96–7, 102–3
Slavs 50–1
Slovakia 51

smallpox 129
Song Dynasty 58
Songhai Empire 66
Soviet Union see USSR
space 107
Space Race 126–7
Spain 47, 54, 73, 81, 82, 117
Spanish Civil War 117
Spanish flu 128, 129
spies 117, 124
Sputnik 1 126
Sri Lanka 110
Stalin, Joseph 117
steam power 104–5
Stone Age 12–13, 20
stone circles 12
Stonehenge 12
stupas 33
submarines 118
suffrage 110–11
Suffragettes 111
Sui Dynasty 58
Süleyman I, Sultan 84–5
sundials 62–3
Swahili culture 69

T
Taj Mahal 86–7
Tang Dynasty 45, 58
tanks 118–19
taxation 92
technology 107, 109, 130

telescopes 78, 127
temples 34–5, 64–5, 73
Tenochtitlan 72–3
Tereshkova, Valentina 127
terracotta warriors 23
Timur 57, 86
tools 12, 20
Toungoo Empire 65
tournaments 53
trade, 18, 19, 24–5, 39, 44–5, 48, 55, 80, 81, 93
Trail of Tears 82
trains 104–5
trench warfare 108–9
tsars 112
Tubman, Harriet 97
Turkey, Ottoman Empire 43, 84–5

U
Ukraine 51
Underground Railroad 96–7
underground trains 104–5
USSR 113, 117, 124–5, 126–7

V
vaccines 129
Vandals 47
Vietnam War 125

Vikings 48–9, 80
viruses 128–9
Visigoths 47
voting 26, 27, 110–11, 122, 123, 131
Voyager 1 127

W
Wales 47
Wall Street Crash 114
Washington, George 92
Wat Lokayasutharam 64
Wat Mahathat 64
water 88
Waterloo, Battle of 95
Western Front 108
Western Roman Empire 43
Wollstonecraft, Mary 110–11
World War One 108–9, 111, 113, 116
World War Two 116, 118–19
World Wide Web 131
Wright, Orville and Wilbur 105
writing 6–7
  China 23, 59
  Cyrillic script 51
  Indus Valley 15
  Olmecs 35
  runic alphabet 47

X
Xerxes I of Persia 28
Xia Dynasty 58

Y
Yuan Dynasty 59
Yup'ik people 71
yurts 56

Z
zeppelins 109
Zhou Dynasty 58, 59
ziggurats 14
Zimbabwe 68–9
Zoroastrianism 28

Acknowledgements

DORLING KINDERSLEY would like to thank: Polly Goodman for proofreading; Helen Peters for the index; Duutan Jamsranjav Gerelbadrakh for his help with pages 56–57; Dr Mihye Harker for her help with pages 60–61; Dr Haifaa Jawad for her help with pages 54–55; Raphael Chijioke Njoku for his help with pages 18–19, 66–69, and 120–121; Taylor Notah for her help with pages 70–71 and 82–83; Verónica Pérez Rodríguez for her help with pages 34–35 and 72–73; Rosemary Sadlier for her help with pages 96–97 and 122–123; Dr Satona Suzuki, lecturer at SOAS University of London, for her help with pages 62–63; and Yilin Wang for her help with pages 22–23 and 58–59.

The publisher would like to thank the following for their kind permission to reproduce their photographs:

(Key: a-above; b-below/bottom; c-centre; f-far; l-left; r-right; t-top)

1 © The Trustees of the British Museum. All rights reserved. 2 The Metropolitan Museum of Art: Gift of Henry G. Marquand, 1881 (bl). **3 © The Trustees of the British Museum. All rights reserved.:** (b). **4 Alamy Stock Photo:** agefotostock / Historical Views (crb); Artokoloro (tr). **5 Dorling Kindersley:** Clive Streeter / The Science Museum, London (cb). **Dreamstime.com:** Fatma Karabacak (bc); Sergey Melnikov (ca). **6–7 Dreamstime.com:** Yuliia Yurasova (t). **6 Alamy Stock Photo:** World History Archive (br). **Dorling Kindersley:** Gary Ombler / Board of Trustees of the Royal Armouries (cra). **Getty Images / iStock:** E+ / eclipse_images (crb). **7 Alamy Stock Photo:** Ian G Dagnall (clb); Pacific Press Media Production Corp. / Michael Debets (cra); PjrStudio (bl). **Canadian Museum of History and Canadian War Museum:** (br/ polar bear). **Dorling Kindersley:** Amit Pashricha / National Museum, New Delhi (cl). **Dreamstime.com:** Jannoon028 (ca/ tablet); Lovelyday12 (ca). **Getty Images:** De Agostini / DEA / G. CIGOLINI (bc). **The Metropolitan Museum of Art:** Gift of William B. Osgood Field, 1902 (br); Gift of Henry G. Marquand, 1881 (fbl). **8 Getty Images / iStock:** E+ / theasis (bl). **8–9 Dreamstime.com:** Dmitry Rukhlenko (t). **9 Alamy Stock Photo:** The Picture Art Collection (tr). **10 Alamy Stock Photo:** Heritage Image Partnership Ltd / Fine Art Images (clb). **Dreamstime.com:** Maximbg (c). **11 Australian National University:** Tim Maloney (bl). **F. d'Errico, D. Rosso:** (clb). **Courtesy of National Park Service, USA:** (cr). **Science Photo Library:** S. Entressangle / E. Daynes (tl). **12 Alamy Stock Photo:** Quagga Media (br); Science History Images (tr). **Getty Images / iStock:** E+ / theasis (cr). **13 Alamy Stock Photo:** North Wind Picture Archives (tl). **Bridgeman Images:** Look and Learn (cl). **Dreamstime.com:** Maximenko50 (tr). **NASA:** (bl). **14 Getty Images / iStock:** fotolinchen (bc). **The Metropolitan Museum of Art:** Purchase, 1886 (bl). **15 Alamy Stock Photo:** World History Archive (br). **16 Dorling Kindersley:** Dan Crisp (cb); Dan Crisp (bc). **16–17 Dreamstime.com:** Claudiodivizia (PaperX5). **17 © The Trustees of the British Museum. All rights reserved.:** (cr). **Dorling Kindersley:** Peter Anderson / Bolton Metro Museum (l). **18 Alamy Stock Photo:** Artokoloro (c); CPA Media Pte Ltd / Pictures From History (br). **18–19 Dreamstime.com:** Deskcube (c). **19 Alamy Stock Photo:** Artokoloro (tc). **Dreamstime.com:** Ingemar Magnusson (bc); Meinzahn (cr). **20 Alamy Stock Photo:** agefotostock / Historical Views (bc); Artokoloro (fbr). **Dorling Kindersley:** Gary Ombler / Newcastle Great Northern Museum, Hancock (cr). **Getty Images:** Hulton Archive / Print Collector / CM Dixon (fcr). **Getty Images / iStock:** Giulia_Schiavi (c). **The Metropolitan Museum of Art:** Bequest of Walter C. Baker, 1971 (br); Gift of Josef and Brigitte Hatzenbuehler, 2007 (fcrb). **21 Alamy Stock Photo:** Artokoloro (cl/cla). **Getty Images:** Hulton Archive / Heritage Images (clb); Sepia Times / Universal Images Group (clb/Bracelet). **22 Alamy Stock Photo:** Robert Kawka (tr); The Picture Art Collection (tl). **Dreamstime.com:** Silvershot55 (tc). **23 Alamy Stock Photo:** MET / BOT (tl); TAO Images Limited / Hongjie Ma (tc). **Dreamstime.com:** Shuo Wang (bc). **Getty Images / iStock:** dndavis (tr). **24 Alamy Stock Photo:** Mike Goldwater (br). **25 Alamy Stock Photo:** Gordon Sinclair (tl). **Science Photo Library:** David Parker (ca). **26 Dreamstime.com:** James Group Studios, Inc. (bl). **27 Dreamstime.com:** Charalambos Andronos (cra). **28 Dreamstime.com:** Vladimir Melnik (bl); Radiokafka (br). **Getty Images:** The Image Bank / Tuul & Bruno Morandi (tl). **29 Alamy Stock Photo:** INTERFOTO / Fine Arts (crb); Science History Images / Photo Researchers (tr). **Shutterstock.com:** Gianni Dagli Orti (clb). **31 Alamy Stock Photo:** incamerastock / ICP (bl). **32 Alamy Stock Photo:** PhotosIndia.com LLC / ImageDB (br). **33 Alamy Stock Photo:** Heritage Image Partnership Ltd (bl). **Dreamstime.com:** Dmitry Rukhlenko (tr). **Shutterstock.com:** krithnarong Raknagn (bc). **34–35 Getty Images / iStock:** SOMATUSCANI (t). **35 Dreamstime.com:** Alexandersr (bc). **36 Dreamstime.com:** Hoang Bao Nguyen (clb). **37 Getty Images:** Hulton Archive / USC Pacific Asia Museum (cr). **38 Alamy Stock Photo:** Lebrecht Music & Arts (br). **38–39 Dreamstime.com:** Tawatchai Prakobkit (t). **40–41 Alamy Stock Photo:** Peter Hermes Furian (c). **41 123RF.com:** Tatyana Borozenets (ca); Tatyana Borozenets (ca/Osiris); Tatyana Borozenets (ca/Sekhmet, ca/Isis). **Alamy Stock Photo:** IanDagnall Computing (tc). **42 Dreamstime.com:** Neurobite (tr). Leu Numismatik AG: (tl). **42–43 Alamy Stock Photo:** Ivy Close Images (c). **43 Alamy Stock Photo:** CPA Media Pte Ltd / Pictures From History (tr). **Dreamstime.com:** Anton Aleksenko (b). **44 Alamy Stock Photo:** North Wind Picture Archives (tc). **45 Alamy Stock Photo:** Peter Horree (bl). **46 Alamy Stock Photo:** Granger - Historical Picture Archive (cl). **Getty Images:** Deagostini / DEA / A. Dagli Orti (br). **47 Alamy Stock Photo:** Azoor Photo (tl); The Print Collector / Heritage Images (tr). **New Forest National Park Authority:** Illustration by Alan Duncan. © 2021 (tc). **48 Alamy Stock Photo:** John Martin Davies (c). **49 Alamy Stock Photo:** GL Archive (tr). **Shutterstock.com:** delcarmat (tl). **Vikings of Middle England:** Alan Kael Ball (c). **51 Alamy Stock Photo:** Ianni Dimitrov Pictures (cr); INTERFOTO / History (c, cl). **52 Alamy Stock Photo:** Studio9 (clb). **53 Alamy Stock Photo:** AC Images (clb); George Brice (br). **Dreamstime.com:** Konstantin Shishkin (bc/crb). **54 Alamy Stock Photo:** imageBROKER / Fabian von Poser (cla); World History Archive (crb). **Dreamstime.com:** Vlad Ghiea (tc). **55 Alamy Stock Photo:** Archivah (bc); Chung Jin Mac (cla); Photo12 / Archives Snark (tc). **Shutterstock.com:** Gianni Dagli Orti (cb). **56–57 Dreamstime.com:** Dmitry Chulov (b); Yongnian Gui. **56 Dreamstime.com:** Viktor Nikitin (clb). **57 Alamy Stock Photo:** Digital Image Library (tr); IanDagnall Computing (tl, tc). **58 Alamy Stock Photo:** GRANGER - Historical Picture Archive (cra); The History Collection (bl); View Stock China (crb). **Dreamstime.com:** Stuart Elflett (cl). **59 Alamy Stock Photo:** Artokoloro (cb); Photo12 / Archives Snark (clb). **Getty Images / iStock:** kool99 (tl). **The Metropolitan Museum of Art:** Rogers Fund, 1926 (bl). **Shutterstock.com:** Zhu Difeng (cra). **60–61 Alamy Stock Photo:** Lebrecht Music & Arts. **61 Alamy Stock Photo:** agefotostock / Historical Views (c). **Dorling Kindersley:** Dave King / Pitt Rivers Museum, University of Oxford (clb). **Dreamstime.com:** Mikeaubry (bl); Noppakun (tc). **62 akg-images:** Heritage Art / Fine Art Images (cl). **Alamy Stock Photo:** Matteo Omied (tc). **62–63 Dreamstime.com:** Zz3701 (c). **63 Alamy Stock Photo:** Uber Bilder (c). **Dreamstime.com:** Miyuki Satake (bl). **64 Dreamstime.com:** Thitipong Kumpusiri (tl); Manit Larpluechai (cra); Tawatchai Prakobkit (clb). **Shutterstock.com:** Adel Newman (br). **65 Alamy Stock Photo:** The History Emporium (cra). **Dreamstime.com:** Ruri Rubiyanto (bl). **66 Alamy Stock Photo:** Artokoloro (clb); John Warburton-Lee Photography / Nigel Pavitt (cl); Sabena Jane Blackbird (bl). **68 Dreamstime.com:** Jo Reason (bl). **69 Dreamstime.com:** Agap13 (tr). **70 Alamy Stock Photo:** David Tipling Photo Library (cr); The Artchives (clb). **Dreamstime.com:** Larry Gevert (br). **71 Alamy Stock Photo:** North Wind Picture Archives (cb); Gary Warnimont (cra). **Shutterstock.com:** Michael Liggett (bc). **73 Dreamstime.com:** Chernetskaya (ca); Katerina Kovaleva (cb); Whpics (tl). **74 Dreamstime.com:** Lopolo (clb). **74–75 Getty Images:** Sawassakorn Muttapraprut / EyeEm. **75 Dreamstime.com:** Noamfein (tr). **76 Alamy Stock Photo:** Chris Hellier (tc). **76–77 Alamy Stock Photo:** Brent Bergherm / DanitaDelimont (t); Dinodia Photos RM (b). **78 Alamy Stock Photo:** Clearview (tc); Historical Images Archive (cl). **Dreamstime.com:** Danflcreativo (cla); Dcslim (cla/Column); Alberto Masnovo (ca). **78–79 Dreamstime.com:** Fatma Karabacak (b). **79 Alamy Stock Photo:** Peter Barritt (tc); Peter Barritt (ca); incamerastock / ICP (cb). **Dorling Kindersley:** Philippe Sebert / Musee du Louvre, Paris (tl). **80 Bridgeman Images:** NPL - DeA Picture Library (crb). **Dreamstime.com:** Sergey Melnikov (bl). **81 Alamy Stock Photo:** Classic Image (cb); Vintage_Space (tc); Universal Art Archive (bl). **Dreamstime.com:** Cupertino10 (tl). **82–83 Alamy Stock Photo:** North Wind Picture Archives. **82 © Johnnie Diacon (Mvskoke):** (bl). **83 Alamy Stock Photo:** Brent Bergherm / DanitaDelimont (tr); GRANGER - Historical Picture Archive (tc/BOW); Pictures Now (tc); North Wind Picture Archives (ftr). **84 Alamy Stock Photo:** Science History Images / Photo Researchers (c); World History Archive (l); Science History Images / Photo Researchers (cr). **85 Alamy Stock Photo:** Art Collection 2 (cl); Chris Hellier (tl); World History Archive (cr). **86–87 Alamy Stock Photo:** Michele Falzone. **86 Alamy Stock Photo:** Dinodia Photos RM (cra); Everett Collection Historical (bl). **87 Alamy Stock Photo:** Miriam Karen Gimbel (cla). **88–89 Alamy Stock Photo:** Travel Pictures / Dallas and John Heaton (t). **88 Alamy Stock Photo:** Antony Baxter (cr); Suzanne Long (br). **89 Alamy Stock Photo:** Auscape International Pty Ltd / Ben Cropp (tr); Auscape International Pty Ltd / Jean-Paul Ferrero (cl). **Getty Images:** Moment / Santiago Urquijo (bl). **90 Alamy Stock Photo:** Everett Collection Inc (br); World History Archive (t). **91 Dorling Kindersley:** Clive Streeter / The Science Museum, London (t). **92 Alamy Stock Photo:** Everett Collection Inc (bl); Geopix (tl); Science History Images / Photo Researchers (tr); North Wind Picture Archives (br). **93 Alamy Stock Photo:** North Wind Picture Archives (tc); The Print Collector / Heritage Images (b). **94–95 Alamy Stock Photo:** Classic Image. **94 Dreamstime.com:** Worldheritage4 (br). **95 123RF.com:** nerthuz (bc). **Alamy Stock Photo:** Album (tl); Prisma Archivo (bl); World History Archive (br). **96 Alamy Stock Photo:** Randy Duchaine (cb). **Dreamstime.com:** Goldghost (bl). **97 Alamy Stock Photo:** Design Pics Inc / Destinations / Tom Patrick (tl); North Wind Picture Archives (cra). **98 Alamy Stock Photo:** North Wind Picture Archives (b); The Granger Collection (br). **98–99 Alamy Stock Photo:** World History Archive. **100 Dreamstime.com:** Airborne77 (cla); Johnfoto (br). **101 123RF.com:** Eric Isselee (crb). **Alamy Stock Photo:** The Print Collector (tl). **Dreamstime.com:** Bborriss (cra); Mahira (clb). **102 Alamy Stock Photo:** Pictures Now (cl); Stocktrek Images, Inc. (tl). **103 Alamy Stock Photo:** Archive Pics (crb); Photo Art Collection (PAC) (tc). **104 Alamy Stock Photo:** Antiqua Print Gallery (bl); Artokoloro (cra); Reading Room 2020 (br); Sueddeutsche Zeitung Photo / Scherl (clb). **105 Alamy Stock Photo:** LOC Photo (tr); World History Archive (ca); World History Archive (cl); Maurice Savage (bl). **Dorling Kindersley:** Clive Streeter / The Science Museum, London (tl). **Shutterstock.com:** Chine Nouvelle / SIPA (br). **106 NASA. 106–107 Alamy Stock Photo:** piemags (b). **Getty Images:** AFP / Gerard Malie / Staff (t). **109 Getty Images:** ND / Neurdein / Roger Viollet (cr). **110 Dreamstime.com:** Dudlajzov (clb). **110–111 Alamy Stock Photo:** Pictorial Press Ltd (t). **Shutterstock.com:** Everett Collection (b). **111 Alamy Stock Photo:** Panther Media GmbH / styleuneed (c); piemags (br). **Getty Images:** Corbis Historical / Hulton Deutsch (tr). **112–113 Alamy Stock Photo:** Everett Collection Historical. **113 Alamy Stock Photo:** Archive Collection (fbr); Photo12 (tc); GL Archive (bl); Lebrecht Music & Arts (bc). **Dreamstime.com:** Ivan Sizov (br). **114 Alamy Stock Photo:** Chronicle (cl); Stocktrek Images, Inc. (clb); World History Archive (bl). **114–115 Alamy Stock Photo:** World History Archive. **116 Alamy Stock Photo:** IanDagnall Computing (tl); Pictorial Press Ltd (tc). **116–117 Getty Images:** ullstein bild / James E. Abbe (t). **117 Alamy Stock Photo:** CBW (tr); GRANGER - Historical Picture Archive (tc); Chronicle (cr); Sueddeutsche Zeitung Photo / Scherl (bc). **118 Alamy Stock Photo:** Asar Studios (crb); dpa picture alliance / Archive / Berliner Verlag (clb); GL Archive (bl). **Dorling Kindersley:** Gary Ombler / RAF Museum, Cosford (tr); The Tank Museum, Bovington (cra); Gary Ombler / Scale Model World (br). **119 Alamy Stock Photo:** piemags (bl). **Dorling Kindersley:** Gary Ombler / Royal Airforce Museum, London (tl). **Dreamstime.com:** Alexander Tolstykh (cla). **NARA & DVIDS Public Domain Archive:** (clb). **120 Alamy Stock Photo:** INTERFOTO / Personalities (clb). **120–121 Alamy Stock Photo:** Dinodia Photos RM (b); The Picture Art Collection (t). **121 Alamy Stock Photo:** Dinodia Photos RM (br); Sueddeutsche Zeitung Photo / Scherl (tr). **Dreamstime.com:** Liligraphie (c). **122 Alamy Stock Photo:** Alpha Historica (bl); GRANGER - Historical Picture Archive (br). **122–123 Alamy Stock Photo:** GRANGER - Historical Picture Archive. **123 Alamy Stock Photo:** Geopix (bc); White House Photo (br). **Shutterstock.com:** Uncredited / AP (bl). **124 Alamy Stock Photo:** SuperStock / Camera Press / Sydney Morning Herald (c). **Dreamstime.com:** Andegraund548 (bl); Pavle Matic; Vladimir Velickovic (crb). **Getty Images / iStock:** MaksimYremenko (bc). **125 Alamy Stock Photo:** Cola Images (cl). **Dreamstime.com:** Fabrizio Mariani (crb); Petro Perutskyy (bl); Okchit; StockNinjaStudio (cb/Flag); Oleg Nikiforov (cb); Oleg Nikiforov (br). **Getty Images:** AFP / Gerard Malie / Staff (cra). **126 Getty Images:** Universal Images Group / Sovfoto (clb). **126–127 NASA. 127 Alamy Stock Photo:** Pictorial Press Ltd / Roscosmos (ca); UPI / NASA (bc). **NASA. 128 Alamy Stock Photo:** Everett Collection Historical (tr); Stocktrek Images, Inc. (tl); GRANGER - Historical Picture Archive (tc). **Dreamstime.com:** Joyfull (c). **129 Alamy Stock Photo:** GRANT ROONEY PREMIUM (c); Science History Images / Photo Researchers (bl). **Dreamstime.com:** Valentin Ayupov (br); Lacheev (tr); Whpics (bc/smallpox); Satori13 (bc). **130 Alamy Stock Photo:** Science History Images / Spencer Sutton (crb). **Dreamstime.com:** Kittipong Jirasukhanont (clb). **131 Alamy Stock Photo:** Science History Images (tl); Michael Wheatley (crb). **Dreamstime.com:** Fizkes (tc). **Getty Images / iStock:** maystra (clb). **Shutterstock.com:** Panthere Noire (tr). **132 Shutterstock.com:** krithnarong Raknagn (bl). **133 The Metropolitan Museum of Art:** Rogers Fund, 1926 (br). **134 Alamy Stock Photo:** Peter Hermes Furian (crb); Heritage Image Partnership Ltd (l). **Vikings of Middle England:** Alan Kael Ball (cr). **134–135 Dreamstime.com:** Bo Li. **135 Alamy Stock Photo:** North Wind Picture Archives (tl); Photo12 / Archives Snark (tc). **Dorling Kindersley:** Philippe Sebert / Musee du Louvre, Paris (tr). **Dreamstime.com:** Fizkes (clb); Mikeaubry (cl); Panpreeda Mahalee (bl). **136 Dorling Kindersley:** Peter Anderson / Bolton Metro Museum (l). **Getty Images:** Universal Images Group / Sovfoto (cr). **136–137 Dreamstime.com:** Bo Li; Tawatchai Prakobkit (b). **137 Alamy Stock Photo:** AC Images (tl); LOC Photo (ca); GRANT ROONEY PREMIUM (cb); GRANGER - Historical Picture Archive (crb). **Dreamstime.com:** Fatma Karabacak (cra). **140 Getty Images:** De Agostini / DEA / G. CIGOLINI (bl). **The Metropolitan Museum of Art:** Purchase, 1886 (bc). **Shutterstock.com:** delcarmat (br). **141 Alamy Stock Photo:** World History Archive (bl). **Shutterstock.com:** Chine Nouvelle / SIPA (br). **142–143 Dorling Kindersley:** Gary Ombler / RAF Museum, Cosford (b). **142 The Metropolitan Museum of Art:** Gift of Josef and Brigitte Hatzenbuehler, 2007 (bl). **143 The Metropolitan Museum of Art:** Gift of William B. Osgood Field, 1902 (bc)

Endpaper images: *Front & Back:* **Getty Images / iStock:** dndavis

Cover images: *Front:* **123RF.com:** salamatik c/ (Copper); **Alamy Stock Photo:** Ian G Dagnall cl, Lebrecht Music & Arts tc, World History Archive bl; **Dorling Kindersley:** Gary Ombler / Royal Airforce Museum, London cra, Clive Streeter / The Science Museum, London cla; **Dreamstime.com:** Claudiodivizia, Dudlajzov tr/ (Memorial), Maor Glam / Glamy tr, Mopic c, Ivan Sizov crb; **The Metropolitan Museum of Art:** Gift of Josef and Brigitte Hatzenbuehler, 2007 crb/ (Armband), Purchase, 1886 tl; **Shutterstock.com:** delcarmat cr/ (mythology); *Back:* **123RF.com:** Tatyana Borozenets crb; **Alamy Stock Photo:** Artokoloro tr, Everett Collection Historical cla, View Stock China clb; **Dreamstime.com:** Claudiodivizia, Peter Hermes Furian cra, Sergey Melnikov cr; **The Metropolitan Museum of Art:** Gift of Henry G. Marquand, 1881 tl, Gift of William B. Osgood Field, 1902 cl; *Spine:* **Dreamstime.com:** Peter Hermes Furian ca

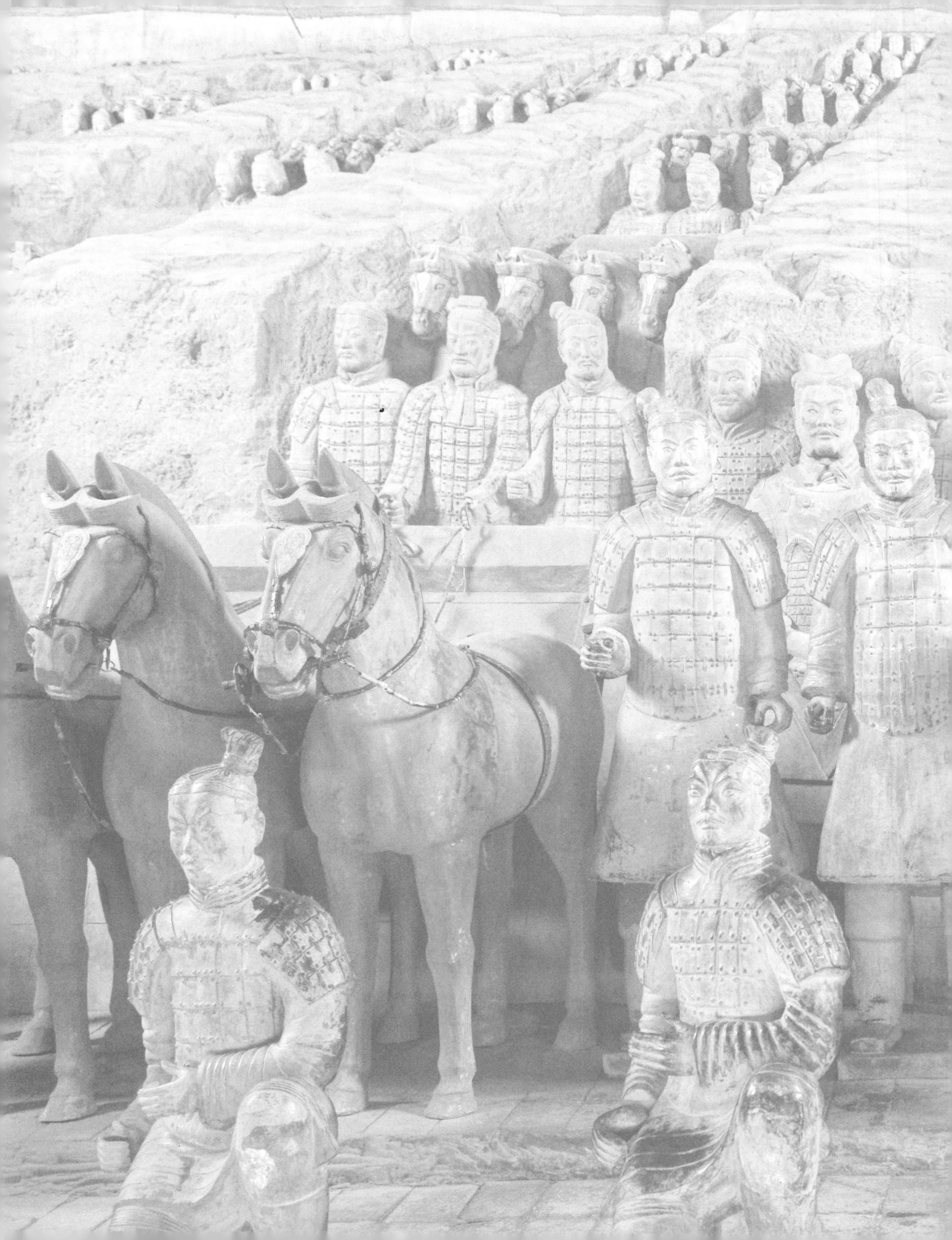